Is it insensitive
to share your faith?

Is it insensitive to share your faith?

Hard questions about Christian mission
in a plural world

James R. Krabill

Intercourse, PA 17534
800/762-7171
www.GoodBks.com

Acknowlegments

Photography by the author: front cover, pages 14, 37, 125, 136, 144.

Grateful acknowledgement is made to the following for permission to reprint: An excerpt from "In Search of the Sacred" from *Newsweek*, November 28, 1994. © 1994 Newsweek, Inc. All rights reserved. Reprinted by permission. An excerpt from *Community and Commitment* by John Driver. © 1976 by Herald Press, Scottdale, PA 15683. Used by permission. An excerpt from *Living Like Jesus* by Ronald J. Sider. © 1996 by Baker Books, a division of Baker Publishing Group. Used by permission.

Design by Dawn J. Ranck

Library of Congress Cataloging-in-Publication Data

Krabill, James R.
  Is it insensitive to share your faith? : hard questions about Christian mission in a plural world / James R. Krabill.
      p. cm.
  ISBN 1-56148-484-9 (pbk.)
  1. Missions--Theory. 2. Religious pluralism--Christianity. I. Title.
  BV2063.K68 2005
  266'.001--dc22   2005007863

To my parents,
Russell and Martha Krabill,
from whom I first learned about Jesus.

Table of Contents

1.
THE PROBLEM:
It's time to call a squirrel, a squirrel

The story is told of a Sunday school teacher who was trying to get a conversation started in her class. She held up a large photo of a squirrel and asked the students, "Now, boys and girls, what do you see in this picture?" Her question was greeted with total silence. And so she asked it again, "Well, what *is* this? What do you see here in this picture?" Finally, a little boy in the back row raised his hand and, squirming and sputtering, blurted out, "Well . . . I think y-y-you probably want us to say *Jesus*, but it looks an awful lot like a *squirrel* to me!"

Sometimes it is important to simply stop fidgeting in our seats and call a squirrel, a squirrel. There are certainly many areas in our personal lives and within our communities and the church where this is not only necessary, but long overdue.

Many questions are being asked about mission today

One of these areas is in our feelings and understandings about mission. I hear, on one hand, a great deal of enthusiasm for increased commitment and involvement in mission as I travel to various Christian communities across North America. Many churches are being totally revitalized as they learn to think beyond themselves to the bigger picture of what God is doing in the world. The possibility of local believers seeing their congregation as a "center of mission," or perhaps, even better, as a faith community wholly "centered on mission," brings fresh energy, purpose, and hope.

On the other hand, there is a degree of discomfort and a pestering uncertainty about the whole mission enterprise—uncertainty about *where* and *with whom* to engage in mission, about *how* such mission should be carried out, and ultimately, about *whether* mission is even appropriate at all in this diverse, multicultural 21st century. One Christian writer, expressing his feelings in an "alternative" newsletter (which has ceased publication), likely speaks for many others when he asserts:

> I am a Christian because it is a part of the Western tradition of religion, and I am also from that tradition. But the longer I live, the more convinced I am that different religions are the different socio-cultural manifestations of the same Creative Spirit at work. After all, why would a loving, all-powerful and jealous deity reveal itself only to a small group of wandering tribespeople, expecting them to spread a rather imperialistic message around the world?
>
> And where is the justice in dooming persons to eternal torment simply because they had the misfortune of

There is a degree of discomfort and a pestering uncertainty about the whole mission enterprise.

being born in an area not yet "penetrated" by this "good news"? Thus, the idea of "converting" to another religion has lost its importance for me. More important is "converting" to a deeper and more meaningful understanding of one's own religious heritage.

The questions raised here are by no means the only ones people are asking. Several years ago I taught a spring semester course at Goshen College, a small Mennonite liberal arts college in northern Indiana. The course, entitled, "Missions—New Millennium," treated many of the issues one might anticipate in such an offering: biblical and theological foundations, religious worldviews, history of missions, cross-cultural communication principles, current strategies for mission, case studies of particular significance, and so on.

What interested me more than what "the scholars" thought about these matters was what *the students* thought. And so, during the very first class period, the 37 participants in the course were divided into small groups to reflect on what questions they wanted to have addressed throughout the semester.

It took no longer than 20 minutes of discussion to produce 144 questions needing attention. Some of these, of course, appeared multiple times in various group reports. But at least 63 distinct questions were identified by this process, and, of that number, 10 in particular seemed to be most on students' minds.

Much of the students' work throughout the remainder of the course was focused on seeking responses to and reporting on these Top Ten Questions:

1. What is most important in missions—meeting the physical needs of people (social action) or sharing the Good News of Jesus (evangelism)?

2. How does one present the gospel without imposing one's own cultural viewpoints?
3. Is Jesus the *only* way?
4. How far away does one need to go to be a missionary?
5. In what ways are the Christian faith and following Jesus at odds with North American culture?
6. What about those who have never heard of Jesus?
7. How does one decide where to evangelize, and what methods are most appropriate in carrying out the task?
8. Is there a place for short-term missions today? If so, what should it be?
9. What will it take to revitalize and motivate less active, traditional churches for mission?
10. What qualifications are required to be a missionary today, and what kind of training is most helpful in preparation?

Our questions are rooted in three realities

One doesn't need to look far to figure out why people are so full of questions about mission in today's world. The principal reasons for our discomfort, I believe, derive from three realities: our *history* is embarrassing, our *worldview* raises serious doubts, and our *encounters* with people of other faiths create a certain uneasiness for us that we haven't figured out how to resolve. A word about each

---

The principal reasons for our discomfort derive from three realities: our history *is embarrassing,* our worldview *raises serious doubts, and* our encounters *with people of other faiths create uneasiness.*

should clarify why these are a particular challenge to the church today.

Our history is embarrassing. There is no critique of Christian mission I hear more often than this one: "But look at all the nasty stuff that's been done to people in the name of Christ! How can you support mission in the face of such a checkered past?"

Well, there's no doubt about it. Plenty happened in our past that can't and shouldn't make the Christian church proud in any way. I have been so plagued by this issue that I've kept a file for over 25 years entitled, "Lest I forget." Into that file I have dumped scores of stories that represent for me the greatest distortions of the Christian message and that continue, right up until the present day, to give the Good News of Jesus a bad name. The following selections from my file speak amply for themselves:

> ***8th-century, northern Europe.*** For 26 years, Charlemagne, king of the Franks, fought the Saxons until finally, at the point of the sword, they agreed to accept his rule and his faith. "Any unbaptized Saxon," he declared, "who attempts to hide himself among his own people and refuses to accept baptism shall be put to death." It is recorded that on one single day Charlemagne massacred 4,500 Saxons.

> ***1099, Jerusalem.*** Christian Crusaders arrived in Jerusalem, capturing the city for the Church. In a final drive to rid the place of "infidels," the soldiers rounded up the Jewish population, chased them into their houses of worship, and then lit the buildings on fire. When small children were discovered attempting to escape the flames, the soldiers captured them, threw them up into the air, and caught them on their swords. All this

was done while the troops marched in formation around the enflamed buildings, singing, "Christ, We Do All Adore Thee."

1495, the Caribbean. The son of Christopher Columbus reported on a skirmish he had witnessed in the Caribbean: "The soldiers mowed down dozens with point-blank volleys, loosed the dogs to rip open limbs and bellies, chased fleeing Indians into the bush to skewer them with sword and pike, and with God's aid soon gained a complete victory."

Early 1500s, Spain. Columbus petitioned the king and queen of Spain with these words, "I hope in our Lord that Your Highnesses will determine to send priests in great diligence in order to unite to the Church such great populations and to convert them, just as Your Highnesses have destroyed those who were unwilling to confess the Father, the Son and the Holy Spirit."

16th century, Portugal. The words of an anonymous conquistador: "Who can deny that the use of gunpowder against pagans is the burning of incense to our Lord?"

1890, Germany. Chancellor von Caprivi surveyed one of the German colonies in Africa and recommended this action: "We should begin by establishing a few stations in the interior, from which both the merchant and the missionary can operate. Gun and Bible should go hand in hand."

1976, Washington, D.C. Thirty Protestant leaders, many of them household names because of their international radio and TV ministries, met with President Ford at the White House, at their own request, to express concern over lagging U.S. military strength. They

> *It is reported that an American fighter pilot painted in large letters on a bomb he dropped over Baghdad, "If Allah doesn't answer, ask for Jesus."*

noted that whenever the U.S. appears weak, it becomes difficult for them to function overseas. But when America is perceived as militarily strong, it is easier for them to carry out their ministries without harassment.

1991, Persian Gulf. It is reported that an American fighter pilot painted in large letters on a bomb he dropped over Baghdad, "If Allah doesn't answer, ask for Jesus."

2003, South Africa. A church leader in Cape Town expressed concern about Christian witness to Muslim people around the world. "We have always seen the Americans as leading the way in missionary passion and practice," he said. "But the mounting hostility in the Muslim world to Americans and to their perceived modern-day crusade against Islam, has reached such a peak in recent months that it will no doubt make it almost impossible for them to imagine meaningful ministry among Muslims for at least the next generation. If ministry to the Islamic world has any future, it may well be up to Christians from other parts of the world to make it happen."

Our worldview raises doubts. It should not surprise us, I suppose, that many people in the world today have grown weary of the violence brought on by fanatic faiths and bloodied believers. "Imagine there's no religion,"

> *"Imagine there's no religion," crooned John Lennon in the 1970s, "imagine . . . living life in peace."*

crooned John Lennon in the 1970s, "imagine . . . living life in peace."

It may well have been this same sense of general fatigue that characterized "Christian" Europe as it crawled painfully out of the devastating religious wars of the 17th century and into the 18th century of the Enlightenment. Most people were indeed ready for some "enlightenment." Hundreds of thousands, perhaps even millions, of European Christians—both Catholic and Protestant—had lost their lives in conflicts that just wouldn't end. Whole cities, villages, farmsteads, and properties had either disappeared or been destroyed. Many people felt that the quarrels of the century past had arisen from trying to make people believe too much too intensely. The time had come to lighten up, to back away from all the rage, and to turn toward reason.

And so Reason it would be. Where the Church had failed, Reason would prevail. Out with superstition; in with objectivity. Goodbye dogma; hello discovery. Gone divine providence in holding the moon and stars in place; enter human confidence in the awesome, endless capacity of the scientific mind to understand and explain the universe in all its complex, interrelated parts.

None of this, of course, happened over night. In fact, many of the early contributors to what became known as the Enlightenment movement wanted nothing more than to make Christianity stronger by stripping it of that which had caused wars and persecutions. And in the process they hoped to rid it of those beliefs that critical minds found hard to accept.

Yet the prevailing spirit of the age was a spirit of *doubt*— doubt about God's providence (challenged by Newton's theory of gravity), about creation and human nature (questioned by Darwin's theory of evolution), about the purpose and goal of history (redefined by Marx's economic determinism), and about faith and religious experience itself (undermined by Freud's psychological explanations and analyses).

The intellectual legacy of Newton, Darwin, Marx, Freud and other thinkers has shaped us and our Western culture far more than we can ever imagine. Positively, it has made us inquisitive about our universe and contributed to some of the most remarkable discoveries and creative inventions

IDEOLOGY	TIME	BELIEF
Biblical Morality ↓	1800-early 1900s	"Certain things are right and wrong, and I know why."
Abiblical Morality ↓	1900-1950s	"Certain things are right and wrong, but I don't know why."
Immorality ↓	1960s-early 1970s	"Certain things are right and wrong, but I don't care!"
Amorality	late 1970s-present	"There's no such thing as right and wrong!"

Adapted from Fran Sciacca, *Generation at Risk* (Minneapolis: World Wide Publications, 1990), p. 113.

> *Matters of faith and religion can neither be tested nor proven in a laboratory. They must therefore either be classified as nonexistent or reduced to the realm of private, personal beliefs.*

the world has ever seen. I am keenly aware of this central theme in our culture every time I attend the Science Fair at the elementary school where my wife teaches third grade. Touring the various projects, I find 10-12-year-olds holding forth on themes like, "The Effects of Driveway Salt on Earthworms," "Which Materials Make the Best Insulators," and "Exploring Whether Rotten Food Produces Gas." (I thought we already *knew* this one, but I guess nothing should keep us from trying to figure out why, in what way, how much, and for how long!)

There is, however, a backside to this process of scientific inquiry that has markedly shaped the way we think—a process that has rigorously trained our minds to reason, often unconsciously, along these lines:

1. **It all starts in the lab.** Everything—all reality—must be submitted to investigative scrutiny with the use of accredited laboratory testing methods and devices in order to be proven "real" or "true."

2. **Only what's "real" survives.** Anything unable to pass this test is considered "not real"—likely unbelievable, possibly nonexistent, certainly unacceptable—and must be taken out of the realm of public scientific discourse and placed under the lower-ranking label of private discourse or personal opinion.

3. **Religion goes private.** Matters of faith and religion can neither be tested nor proven in a laboratory. They must therefore either be classified as nonexistent or reduced to the realm of private, personal beliefs.

4. **It's all about "me."** Since religious matters are nothing more than one's own private affair or personal opinion, they really don't apply to anyone other than . . . me.

5. **Anything goes.** If this is true, then each individual or group is both free and encouraged to adopt or develop, without the slightest judgment or critique, whatever belief systems or codes of moral behavior they might choose. Anything and everything is acceptable, and all is of equal value for life in this world and the next—should there turn out to be one.

6. **Forget the common story.** There is, of course, in such a case, no common story, no "meta-narrative" linking or holding together all the smaller, personal stories.

7. **You go your way and I'll go mine.** And, consequently, it would not only be stupid, rude, and presumptuous, but ultimately inconceivable, to imagine why one might "share" one's own personal story, or, worse yet, "impose" it on anyone else.

Our encounters with other faiths create unease. There was a time when none of this would have mattered much, a time when it was rare in most of mainstream America to meet someone whose worldview differed greatly from one's own.

During my earliest childhood years in the small, midwestern town of Goshen, Indiana, encountering someone of a different faith meant getting to know Butch, the only Roman Catholic in my otherwise-Protestant elementary school

About 15 percent of the current U. S. population claims to belong to religions other than Christianity.

class. Though I sensed from classmates and others that there was something slightly different about Butch, I never got the opportunity to find out what that was before his parents moved him out of my life and into the Catholic parochial school on the other side of town.

The religious and ethnic composition of America's population up until the mid-1960s was shaped largely by rather strict immigration laws that favored Europeans (mostly Christian, a few Jewish) and small numbers of Canadians and Mexicans, neighbors across the borders to the north and south.

That all changed dramatically with the Immigration Act of 1965 which opened up large-scale immigration from other parts of the world. Asian immigrants had never before exceeded more than five percent of the new arrivals, but between 1960-84 that number rose to over 30 percent. Principal here were those coming from the Philippines, Korea, Vietnam, China, Laos, Cambodia, and India, bringing with them their beliefs and practices rooted firmly in Buddhism, Hinduism, and various other East Asian religions.

Added to these in more recent years have been large numbers of African and Middle Eastern arrivals, all contributing to the ever-expanding religious smorgasbord found in America today. About 15 percent of the current U. S. population claims to belong to religions other than Christianity. Muslims now outnumber Presbyterians, Buddhists have surpassed Assembly of God members, and Hindus can be found in greater number than Episcopalians.

Though we have grown accustomed to expecting increased diversity in the lives of those around us, most Christians are still somewhat disoriented and largely ill-prepared when:

• They browse through the yellow pages of their local phone book and find listings for the Ba'hai Task Force, the Sikh Study Circle, Vendanta the Eternal Quest, and the Vietnamese Buddhist Association.

• Their daughter in college brings a Muslim boyfriend home for the Christmas holidays.

• A work colleague from India invites them over to the house to celebrate her son's *upanayana*—a Hindu ceremony marking initiation into adulthood.

The questions that arise from these inter-faith encounters tumble out of our heads almost as fast as we can formulate them: So what *is* so unique about Christianity anyway? How can we be so sure that all paths to God aren't the same? Isn't being sincere good enough? Who am I to say what's right and wrong? Doesn't it all come down to geography in the end? I mean, if I had been born in Algeria rather than in America, the chances of me being a Christian wouldn't be very great, would they? Whose fault is *that*?

What I find most amazing about all of this is the small percentage of church life actually devoted to grappling with these difficult issues. Week after week Christians gather for a few hours to "confess their faith in the Risen Lord." Then they return on Monday to the work-a-day world, wondering what the deeper implications of this affirmation are, and what, in fact, this faith has to do with the faiths of their non-Christian friends and colleagues whom they have come to know and appreciate.

We all have deep and unanswered questions about how we ought to live and talk about our faith as Christians. Most of us never express these questions or even admit that we have them. Still fewer of us attempt to answer them.

That is why it is time to call a squirrel, a squirrel. Not because in so doing, all the hard questions will finally go away. But precisely because only then will they finally get openly and honestly asked.

2.
THE COSMIC PLAN:
Does God's "big idea" still apply?

I remember as a high school senior in the late 1960s attending an evening public lecture in a local church with four of my buddies. The presentation was entitled, "Ten Irrefutable Proofs for the Existence of God." The gentleman holding forth that night was a visiting professor from a midwestern Bible college. He had spent over 15 years writing books and giving presentations designed to help Christians defend their faith, if and when confronted by atheists, agnostics, or any other kind of secularized unbeliever.

The guy was good. Pulling arguments out of his hat from history, philosophy, science, and a bunch of other disciplines I had never heard of, he made the case for why it was more logical, more rational, more reasonable, more . . . *everything,* to believe in the existence of God than to doubt it.

My friends and I were naïve and cocky enough to take him on. We cornered him at the end of the presentation and extended the session for another full hour of impassioned debate. In the end, however, he creamed us. He was just too good—too logical, too rational, too *everything*—and we came away knowing we had been soundly routed by the guy's overwhelming and incontestable arguments from empirical evidence.

First there was no God

On many occasions in the years following, the lively debate of that evening came back to me. One of those moments was in 1972 when I visited L'Abri, a retreat-study center in Switzerland, founded by Francis Schaeffer for the very purpose of engaging a generation of doubters with just such questions. Schaeffer was best known in those days for his books, *Escape from Reason, The God Who Is There,* and his just-released publication, *He Is There and He Is Not Silent,* which dealt with "the philosophic necessity of God's being there and not being silent, in the areas of metaphysics, morals and epistemology."

L'Abri was filled with youthful seekers who had descended upon the center from all over the world to pursue questions and engage in debates of every kind. One unforgettable exchange I had during my stay there lasted nearly eight hours, beginning at the breakfast table and continuing until late afternoon. My conversation partner was a Jewish-born, Marxist-atheist university student who had no time or place for God and was quite convinced that the only driving force at work in the world was people's insatiable thirst for money. "Don't kid yourself," I remember him arguing. "Abraham didn't leave his home in Ur to sacrificially follow God. Spiritual quest had nothing to do with it. Abraham was chasing after 'milk and honey' like everyone else."

Another personal encounter I had with the powerful influence of secularized Western culture came four years later in Paris, France, when Jeanette and I were studying French in preparation for our upcoming African assign-

> *"Don't kid yourself," I remember him arguing. "Abraham didn't leave his home in Ur to sacrificially follow God. Spiritual quest had nothing to do with it. Abraham was chasing after 'milk and honey' like everyone else."*

ment. One of my classmates there was a university student from Japan who, according to his own testimony, had come all the way to France from his home country to learn to read, "in the original mother tongue," the works of his life-long mentor, French existentialist philosopher Jean-Paul Sartre.

Now Sartre was not the most hopeful character around whom to organize one's life and energies. Sartre believed that the ultimate motive for all human behavior was the desire to achieve perfect self-sufficiency—"to become God," he sometimes said—by becoming the cause of one's own existence. Because this goal is actually self-contradictory and impossible to attain, and because there is no God other than in one's own desire and imagination, all human activity is ultimately futile. "Man is a useless passion," he said. "Every existing thing is born without reason, prolongs itself out of weakness, and dies by chance."

When I told my friend that this was not nearly enough to get me out of bed in the morning, he remained undeterred. And when he discovered that Sartre was actually living in the very housing block where our classes were being held, he was ecstatic beyond belief.

In time, we learned that the then-71-year-old gentleman would occasionally make his way down from his apartment to the corner café on Boulevard du Montparnasse and Boulevard Raspail during the late afternoon hours. And so by no later than 4:00 p.m. each and every day, my friend would take his position at a corner table, watching and waiting for a glimpse of his *maître* (his "master," as he reverently referred to him). I was with him on the first day that "it happened." "I can go back to Japan now," he told me. But he didn't. He finished out the year, soaking up as many of these silent encounters as he could and finally even speaking briefly with Sartre when he felt his French-language proficiency had become "worthy of the master."

Then there were too many gods

There is no way to describe adequately the contrast my wife and I experienced when we left France at the end of our studies in 1978 and headed for Ivory Coast, West Africa. On my third day as a Bible teacher in the village of Yocoboué, where we lived for almost four years, an elderly gentleman raised his hand in class and said, "Okay, I have a question for you. There is something I have never understood about the celebration of Holy Communion. Here in the village we live daily with the reality of witches who thrive and survive only because they drink the

> *"Americans have become picky. They demand— and get—what they want, how they want it. Consider: Starbucks offers more than 19,000 ways to order a cup of coffee."*
>
> — Bruce Horowitz
> *USA Today* (March 5-7, 2004)

blood and eat the flesh of other family members they wish to destroy. So now we say that Jesus is our best friend. Why is it, then, that we would want to harm or kill this good friend of ours by drinking his blood and eating his flesh?"

I have never really tried, but I am quite certain I could count on one hand the number of Africans I have met over the years who doubted the existence of God. The issue is generally not *whether* there's a God, but *how many!* Technically speaking, most West Africans believe there is one principal Creator God—but this God presides over a world thoroughly permeated by countless other spiritual forces and beings, from nature and ancestral spirits to clairvoyants, mediums, diviners, and healers. Even objects, otherwise "inanimate" to the naked eye, can become "animated" by people specially gifted with the capacity to transform "things" into powerful forces for good or evil.

Twenty-five years ago, Paris and Yocoboué seemed worlds apart. And in many ways they were. In recent years, however, things have begun to change. Peter Berger, a sociologist of religion, calls this change "the desecularization of the world." Says Berger, in a book by the same title, "The assumption that we live in a secularized world is false. The world today . . . is as furiously religious as it ever was, and in some places more so than ever."

I became particularly aware of this significant cultural shift in 1994 when I was browsing through the magazine section of an Abidjan (Ivory Coast) bookstore and picked up the November 28 issue of *Newsweek*, with its six-page feature story, "In Search of the Sacred." The article described the cafeteria-style spirituality beginning to emerge in North America and illustrated this trend by recounting the spiritual journey of 50-year old Rita McClain. On page 39 of the article, the writer reported:

Rita McClain's spiritual journey began in Iowa, where she grew up in the fundamentalist world of the Pentecostal Church. What she remembers most about that time are tent meetings and an overwhelming feeling of guilt. In her 20s she tried less doctrinaire Protestantism. That, too, proved unsatisfying.

By the age of 27, McClain had rejected all organized religion. "I really felt like a pretty wounded Christian," she says. For the next 18 years, she sought inner peace only in nature, through rock climbing in the mountains or hiking in the desert. That seemed enough.

Then; six years ago, in the aftermath of an emotionally draining divorce, McClain's spiritual life blossomed. Just as she had once explored mountains, she began scouting the inner landscape. She started with Unity, a metaphysical church near her Marin County, Calif., home. It was a revelation, light-years away from the "Old Testament kind of thing I knew very well from my childhood."

The next stop was Native American spiritual practices. Then it was Buddhism at Marin County's Spirit Rock Meditation Center, where she has attended a number of retreats, including one that required eight days of silence.

These disparate rituals melded into a personal religion, which McClain, a 50-year-old nurse, celebrates at an ever-changing altar in her home. Right now the altar consists of an angel statue, a small bottle of "sacred water" blessed at a women's vigil, a crystal ball, a pyramid, a small brass image of Buddha sitting on a brass leaf, a votive candle, a Hebrew prayer, a tiny Native American basket from the 1850s and a picture of her "most sacred place," a madrone tree near her home.

> *There is no doubt that these new forms of spiritual quest are custom-made for the mix 'em, match 'em salad-bar consumer culture of North America.*

Charles Strohmer, writer and lecturer on current religious trends, calls experiences like Rita's "The New Spirituality"—a swirl of beliefs and practices inspired by elements of Eastern religions, New Age-ism, self-help and pop psychologies, the occult, and "a dash of Western optimism" bolstered by "whatever current scientific theories can be assumed."

However one might choose to assess this new form of spiritual quest, there is no doubt that it is custom-made for the mix 'em, match 'em salad-bar consumer culture of North America. What the New Spirituality has to offer is, of course, what Americans love most: the opportunity and freedom to choose from a wide range of options in designing a "product" that suits their needs.

In spiritual terms, the *Newsweek* story reported that Rita practiced "disparate rituals" from various religious traditions that eventually "melded into a personal religion." A *personal* religion? Hmmm! That should sound familiar, because that is precisely what results—as suggested in the last chapter—when religious matters become one's own private affair or personal opinion. Put most simply: Rita's *religion* is, in the end . . . *Rita's* religion. It is her own personal story after all, her own unique experience, unparalleled and incomparable to anyone else's.

That is why, when asked about the number of religions in America today, I am more and more inclined to reply:

"Why, 288 million, of course. One for every freedom-loving citizen in search of life, liberty and the pursuit of happiness. It's the American way!"

One *faith,* one *hope,* one *God . . . how crazy can you get?*

Just in case we are tempted to think that 21st-century folk are exceptionally gifted in the creation of things religious, we should be reminded that all of this sounds remarkably similar to life and thought in the Greco-Roman world of 2,000 years ago. It is difficult to know exactly how many cults and religions were practiced at that time. But what *is* clear is that temples and statues dedicated to at least a dozen major gods could be found in virtually every urban center throughout the empire. In the crossroads city of Corinth, for example, there were places of worship for Apollo (god of light, purity, and the sun), Poseidon (god of the sea), Aphrodite (goddess of love and fertility), Tyche (goddess of good fortune), Asclepius (god of healing), and the Greek and Egyptian mystery cults of Kore, Demeter, Sarapis, and Isis.

In addition to these there were, of course, a myriad smaller deities of the pocket-size variety: family-owned and village-based powers and protectors, the widely-embraced imperial cult, and countless other oracles, rituals, mystery religions, and philosophies, often imported from foreign lands by sojourners, soldiers, sailors, and slaves.

It was into this "bewildering mass of religious alternatives," as historian E. R. Dodd calls it, that a bunch of crazy people stepped forward to make some crazy claims. "There is but *one* Lord and *one* Spirit," they said, "*one* body, *one* hope, *one* faith, *one* baptism, and *one* God and Father of the entire human race, who is Lord of all, works through all, and is in all" (adapted from Ephesians 4:4-6).

> *It was into this "bewildering mass of religious alternatives," that a bunch of crazy people stepped forward to make some crazy claims.*

How outrageous is that? And it doesn't end there either, they said. This God is the God, not just of our individual family clan, our tribe, or our nation, but of *all* families, tribes, and nations. And this God has a plan. A very BIG plan. A plan to make peace and set things right with the world. The *whole* world. Well, actually, the whole *universe*—all things in deepest heaven, all things on planet earth.

This, they said, is because the God, who in the beginning made all things, is not only a Creator God, but also a Missionary God. How else can one explain why, from the earliest pages of human history when men and women turned their backs on God's love, God took the initiative to pursue them? Why else did God come into their world, seeking, wooing, calling, and restoring them?

God has done this, they said, not because rebellious men and women deserved to be delivered from the terrible mess they had managed to create for themselves, but because this is in the very nature of the Creator's love. And that is why, even before the world began, God put in motion a comprehensive, long-range plan to "bring everything together in Christ."

Speaking of Christ . . . Christ is at the very heart, they said, of God's big plan. You take him out of the picture, and the project falls apart. For it is in Christ, they believed, that everything will be brought together and summed up. In Christ that "all creation will be set free from its slavery to decay" and "brought back to God." That past sins will be forgiven and forever forgotten. That the walls of anger and hostility between countries, clans, and classes will be brought down. And that races living in conflict will be formed into one new people and enter together into God's presence "by Christ's atoning death on the cross."

Okay, some pretty heady concepts there. But it all boils down to one simple point: The earthly life of Jesus, his ministry, death, resurrection, and return to heaven, together constitute the single most important event of all time, the event by which all history is divided and all other events are defined and understood.

That is why those crazy people—sometimes referred to as the Early Church—chose to speak of *one* Lord, not two, ten, or a ton. What could any other Lord possibly do or be that would surpass the All-Sufficient Christ? Hard to imagine. And so, until further notice, the church chose to live— and die—by their unfailing allegiance to the cosmic project God had initiated in Christ Jesus, their . . . *LORD*.

That is then, this is now

When the Apostle Paul stood up in the god-clogged city of Athens and attempted to engage the intellectuals of his day with some of these ideas, the reaction from the crowd

---

The earthly life of Jesus, his ministry, death, resurrection, and return to heaven, together constitute the single most important event of all time, the event by which all history is divided and all other events are defined and understood.

was predictable. "What is this ignorant show-off trying to say," some of them scoffed, or, "What an airhead!" as Eugene Peterson renders it in *The Message*.

We should not be surprised, then, if reactions from people we meet today are somewhat similar to those encountered by Paul during his guest appearance on the Mars Hill Talk Show in Athens almost 2,000 years ago. What I find more intriguing, however, is the degree to which we Christians are shaped by the all-pervasive values and perspectives of the current cultural context in which we live.

In this connection, there are a number of questions I believe it is worth asking as we reflect on the meaning of God's ongoing work in today's world. For example:

- To what extent is God still working on a cosmic project of "bringing all things together in Christ"? Or has God reduced the scope of the project in our day to focus on more limited national, family, or private initiatives?

- To ask it another way: Aside from "my story" and "your story," is there a "God story" that in some significant way still applies to all people in all times and places?

- What are the implications for the church if God's big plan is still in place? Or what, on the other hand, are the implications if God has abandoned the *cosmic* project and gone *local*?

- And how does Jesus fit in to all of this? How important is it that he remains centrally connected to the project God is working on?

- If Jesus really is at the heart of God's project, is it possible for the Christian church to maintain its integrity and work on the project with people of other faiths who aren't so sure about Jesus? If, on the other hand, Jesus' central place in the project is downplayed or eliminated altogether, is it still, in fact, God's project we're working on?

These are by no means the only questions one might have concerning these matters, but they are important ones, and ones to which we will return again in the chapters to follow.

3.

JESUS:
Liar, lunatic, or Lord—What's your final answer?

"That's the spot. That's where it happened," he mumbled almost inaudibly under his breath. My eyes searched the dense forest underbrush along the riverbank for some clue. "That's where . . . *what* happened?" I asked.

Two rivers, two realities, one big question

The year was 1985. For over an hour on this sweltering hot and humid afternoon, I had been drifting silently downstream in a dugout canoe with my traveling companion, "Papa" Robert Dogui, an 82-year-old patriarch, who was accompanying me on an errand from our village of Yocoboué in southcentral Ivory Coast to Tiokossoukrou, a small fishing village some 20 kilometers away.

Over the previous four years, Papa and I had developed a rather deep and abiding friendship. It had all begun one day when he told me, "The youth in our village don't care anymore about the traditions of our people. All they do is chase after loud music, bright lights, and pretty girls. I'm not going to waste my time on them anymore. You are the only person who comes to visit me in my courtyard and asks me questions about our life and culture. I'm going to tell you everything I know."

Everything he knew? Ohhhh! That struck me as a rather scary prospect. From the little experience I had had with Papa, I was quite certain that this would amount to far more information than I could ever handle. "Why do you think old people talk so much?" he twinkled at me one day. "Because they've seen so much in their lifetimes that every story they tell reminds them of another one!" And it was indeed another one of Papa's stories I was about to hear on that sultry day in May of 1985.

"The villages of Yocoboué and Tiokossoukrou," Papa began slowly, "have had a long history of clan wars that date back to a time before human memory. We fought over everything: women, hunting domains, fishing rights. *Everything.* Finally, in the years when my grandfather was still a young lad, the clan leaders came together and said, 'This has got to stop.' And so they made a pact with each other to end the violence, once and for all.

"To seal the pact," Papa continued, "it was agreed that there would need to be a sacrifice. Not an animal sacrifice, as was the usual practice, but a *human* sacrifice—one to which the ancestors of the two villages would be invoked as witnesses, and one which could never be violated or re-

> *"To seal the pact," Papa continued, "it was agreed that there would need to be a sacrifice. Not an animal sacrifice, as was the usual practice, but a human sacrifice."*

tracted in any way without the most dire consequences for the offenders.

"A young teenage virgin was chosen as victim for the sacrifice," said Papa with a growing sense of reverence and intensity in his voice, "and, on the appointed day, she was brought to this spot situated at midpoint between the two villages. It was here that the girl was strung up—head down, legs in the air—and halved with a machete from top to bottom. Each village was then given half of the body to bury when they returned home as a sign of their commitment to end the conflict which had brought so much fear and death to the region."

It was just about four years after this unforgettable canoe trip with Papa Dogui that, in early 1989, I found myself floating down another river. This time I was in Birmingham, England, where I was completing a year-long sabbatical study leave. It was a beautiful Sunday afternoon in the spring of the year, and I was taking a break from the books for a canal ride with my family and a few other friends also involved in the African studies program.

Conversation turned to religion. "Well, I want you to know I'm an atheist," said one of our traveling companions. "But that doesn't keep me from devoting my time to the study of religious beliefs and practices in Africa." "How does that work?" I wanted to know. "It's really quite simple," she said. "Even though I don't personally believe what Africans believe, I know that *they* do, and so I discipline myself to 'see it through their eyes' and to treat what they tell me with utmost respect." (My limited exposure to this scholar's style and treatment of the research data at her disposal indicated to me that she was, in fact, about as fairhanded as they come.)

"I am a researcher," she continued. "It is not my job to *judge* a person's belief, but to *describe* it. People can believe whatever they want to believe as far as I'm concerned. Who am I to tell them that what they're doing is 'right' or 'wrong'?"

My mind flashed back to Papa Dogui's story of the young girl being strung up between two trees down by the riverside. "I must admit I'm curious," I said. "Are you *really* telling me that if you were to come upon a scene in your field research where a young girl was being cut in two for the purpose of ritual sacrifice, you would do nothing more than calmly take a seat as an impartial observer, pull out your notepad and video camera, and proceed to record the event for academic posterity?" "Well, no, of course not," she said. "That is sooo . . . *wrong!*"

Are all *religious beliefs and practices equally good, right, and true?*

We might as well admit it. We have a bit of a problem. No, actually, we have a very big problem.

On one hand, most of us are pretty tired of insensitive, intolerant people flying around trashing and bashing what other people choose to do and believe. There is something very attractive about Mahatma Gandhi's recommendation to "never undermine the faith of others but to make them better followers of their own faiths." Furthermore, everything about our Western culture warms up to Gandhi's statement that "religions are different mountain paths converging to the same point at the peak. What does it matter that we take different paths as long as we reach the same goal? In reality, there are as many different religions as there are individuals."

On the other hand, most of us are equally disturbed by people who, all in the name of religion, go around whacking off other people's body parts, exploiting women and children, presiding over communal sex orgies, and com-

> *Most of us are pretty tired of insensitive, intolerant people flying around trashing and bashing what other people choose to do and believe.*

mandeering commercial airplanes filled with passengers into tall buildings. We are quite convinced, when pushed on the matter, that some religious beliefs and practices are more than mere paths converging at the peak of the mountain. They are, in reality, trails that take you up the mountain . . . and right off the cliff on the other side. They are roads with *dead* ends.

For starters, it is probably good to note that religions are not all the same and, more importantly, don't even claim to be. Why we should claim for religions what they do not claim for themselves is a question at least worth asking. Someone has said, "All religions believe in love and goodness; they only differ on matters of God, creation, sin, salvation, morality, revelation, law, holiness, spirituality, heaven, and hell." Well, yes, that's just the point.

A central affirmation, for example, for most Christians across the ages is that "God has come and is coming again." Our Jewish brothers and sisters, however, see it a bit differently. "God will indeed come someday," many of them would say, "but we are still waiting for that to happen." For most Muslims, "God is wholly transcendent and will, by definition, not be coming." For people embracing certain traditional, ethnic religions, "God has come, was offended by something humans did, and went away angry with no plans to return." For some East Asian religions, "God has 'come,' is everywhere, and is in everything." And for most Western secular atheists, of course, "there is no god to come."

One might well expect that religious understandings as varied as these could, in fact, result in some rather wildly divergent views of the world. You've got that right; they do. And the situation only increases in complexity when one leaves the realm of "mainstream" religious thought to enter the even wilder worlds of people like Bo and Peep, Stewart Traill, and Oric Bovar. Ever met these folks? You need to.

- Bo and Peep formed a movement in 1973 based on their prophecy that they would be assassinated, return from the dead, and leave the planet in a craft from outer space. "Bo" was actually Marshall Herff Applewhite, a musician and opera singer, and "Peep," Bonnie Lu Trousdale Nettles, a professional nurse. In 1997, Applewaite—by then leader of a movement called, "Heaven's Gate"—formed a suicide pact with 38 followers and departed for a "place beyond the confines of the Earth."

- Stewart Traill, a former vacuum-cleaner salesman, founded a group in Pennsylvania called the Forever Family. After opposition arose from parents of "family" members, the group changed its name to the Church of Bible Understanding and moved to New York City where members have been known to stand on street corners soliciting business for the movement's carpet-cleaning company. The group has also done mission work in Haiti.

- In New York, Oric Bovar, a former opera coach who asserted he was the Christ, was found praying over the decomposing body of a follower who had died of cancer. Bovar was charged with failing to report a corpse. On the day he was to stand trial, Bovar jumped from a 10th-floor window and killed himself. He had once said that if he jumped out of a window, God would bounce him back.

I, for one, am not much inclined to warmly affirm the spiritual journeys of the Bo and Peepers, carpet-sweepers, and window-leapers of our world. Nor do I think it would be particularly advisable to encourage the members of these movements to simply "become better followers of their own faiths." This no doubt puts me at odds with Swami Vivekananda, a Hindu spokesperson at the first World's Parliament of Religions, who declared himself proud to belong to a religion that "accepts all religions to be true."

I guess I just can't figure out how that works. Without some kind of standard or reference point by which to evaluate things, how can one affirm with any certainty that Mother Teresa's Sisters of Mercy are more worthy of admiration than, say, Jim Jones' suicidal Jonestown community? Or that David Koresh's Waco compound in Texas serves any less as a model for healthy living than a vibrant house-church fellowship on the south side of Chicago?

When all criteria for assessing religious matters are dismissed as narrow-minded, intolerant, and unacceptable, we then end up in the crazy position described by Beckwith and Koukl in their book on *Relativism*, with our "feet

> *Without some kind of standard or reference point by which to evaluate things, how can one affirm with any certainty that Mother Teresa's Sisters of Mercy are more worthy of admiration than, say, Jim Jones' suicidal Jonestown community?*

firmly planted in mid-air," agreeing to tolerate that which is essentially intolerable and creating a world in which precious few people would want to live.

"I am the way, the truth, and the life" *—words from Jesus that spell relief*

That is why I like to invite people to consider Jesus—the one who enters the religious fray and offers to shed light on what is good, right, and true.

Jesus, of course, does far more than simply offer advice on the matter; he offers *himself* as the best picture of what Goodness and Truth actually look like. "I *AM* the way, the truth, and the life," Jesus declares to his disciples (John 14:6). His assertion is certainly as startling, yet refreshing, in our day as in his, and one that leaves most people wishing for a closer look and a deeper conversation with the man who would dare to make such audacious claims.

Jacob Neusner, author of *A Rabbi Talks with Jesus*, describes what many feel when they encounter Jesus. "Imagine walking on a dusty road in Galilee nearly 2,000 years ago," writes Neusner, "and meeting up with a small band of youngsters, led by a young man. The leader's presence catches your attention: he talks, the others listen, respond, obey—care what he says, follow him. You don't know who the man is, but you know he makes a difference to the people with him and to nearly everyone he meets. People respond, some with anger, some with admiration, a few with genuine faith. But *no one* walks away uninterested in the man and the things he says and does" (*Newsweek*, March 17, 2000: 57).

I once asked an elderly preacher in Ivory Coast how he understood Jesus' claims to be the way, truth, and life. "Ah, that is no small matter!" he told me. "For me to understand Jesus, every part of my body needs to get involved, begin-

The Worrying *or* Pensive Christ—*a frequent depiction of*
Jesus in Lithuanian Christian art.

ning with my head, traveling on to my heart, and right on down to my feet."

I was curious to know what he meant by that. "If I am going to comprehend the *truth* claims Jesus makes," he explained, "my mind needs to think long and hard about what he is saying. If I want to experience the *life* Jesus has to offer, I must open my heart to the peace and joy he wants to give me. And if I want to walk in the *way* of Jesus, I need to get my feet a-movin,' following in the direction he wants to take me."

This dear old brother has set forth in a remarkable way some of the key challenges we face in attempting to *understand, experience,* and *put into practice* what Jesus is calling us to.

The TRUTH about Jesus—training our *minds* to "think clearly." No doubt about it, Jesus makes some rather incredible claims about himself. "All authority in heaven and on earth has been given to me." That's pretty big. But there's much, much more.

- "What I teach is not my own teaching; it comes from God who sent me."

- "If you have seen me, you have seen the one who sent me."

- "You study the Scriptures to find eternal life, but these very Scriptures speak about me."

- "No one comes to the Father except through me."

- "Whoever hears my words and believes in the one who sent me will live forever."

Some of these statements—and there are dozens more—are hard for us to get our heads around. If Jesus is exaggerating here, then he is creating a serious credibility problem for himself. If, on the other hand, his words speak truth, then we're dealing with someone unlike any other in human history.

The LIFE in Jesus—opening our *hearts* to "experience deeply." Encountering Jesus is far more than a head trip. Jesus is indeed *teacher*; he is also *compassionate friend.* "Come to me," he says, "all of you who are tired from carrying heavy loads, and I will give you rest." This loving invitation reminds us that Jesus is interested in more than stimulating our brains; he wants to establish an intimate relationship with us.

- "Remain in me," he counsels, "and I will remain in you."

- "I am the vine, and you are the branches. If you remain in me, and I in you, you will bear much fruit; for you can do nothing without me."

- "I have told you this so that my joy may be in you and that your joy may be complete."

- "And know this—I will be with you always, to the end of the age."

The WAY of Jesus—activating our *feet* to "obey faithfully." Jesus challenges us to believe certain things *about* him. In addition, he courts our friendship and invites us to believe *in* him. Sometimes he asks us to simply . . . *believe him*, by stepping out in obedience and walking in his will and way. "If you love me," he tells his disciples, "you will obey my teaching." To do so will likely land the disciple in a cross-wise position with the surrounding culture.

- "Do not take revenge on someone who wrongs you," says Jesus.

- "Love your enemies and pray for those who persecute you."

- "Do not store up riches for yourself here on earth."

- "Sell all you have and give the money to the poor."

- "Anyone who wants to be great must be a servant of the rest."

- "I am sending you out like sheep to a pack of wolves."

- "Forget self, take up your cross, and follow me."

Many people I meet seem to be drawn to one particular part of Jesus' message, often overlooking or neglecting other aspects of equal importance. And so we have the "thinkers" (who focus on seeking answers to the hard questions), the "feelers" (who emphasize having the right experience) and the "doers" (who insist on putting Jesus' words into action). The danger with this kind of "selective discipleship," however, is its potential to produce intellectuals with no passion, emotionalists with poor grounding, and activists with little joy.

I see no indication anywhere in the life and ministry of Jesus that we've been given the option to pick and choose arbitrarily what we happen to like about Jesus and to leave the rest behind. This approach *would* follow quite nicely

> *I see no indication anywhere in the life and ministry of Jesus that we've been given the option to pick and choose arbitrarily what we happen to like about Jesus and to leave the rest behind.*

the pattern of the culture in which we live, but it doesn't seem to fit the style of the One to whom "all authority in heaven and earth has been given." Jesus didn't suffer and die for only half the cause. So, what, then, are we to make of Jesus—his claims, his compassion, his call for us to follow? After all has been said and done, Jesus comes to us with one essential question—the same one he popped to his first band of disciples nearly 2,000 years ago—"Who then do *you* say that I am?"

Is Jesus "one among the many" or "the One among many"?

People in our day have found many ways to respond to Jesus' question. Some of the most commonly held views are the following.

- **LEGEND: Jesus never lived.** A recent survey in Britain reveals that nearly half the youth there believe Jesus is a fictitious figure who never actually existed.

- **LOST: Jesus is unknowable to us.** Jesus did actually exist as a living person, but there is, unfortunately, no way to peel off the multiple encrusted layers of what others have said and thought about him. Even the New Testament documents tell us far more about the gospel writers and the early church than they do about Jesus. What we actually know of him is minimal, if anything at all.

- **LUDICROUS: Jesus is incomprehensible to modern-day people.** It is possible, perhaps even likely, that Jesus was a wonderful first-century teacher, but much of his ministry and message is unintelligible in our modern scientific age. Once you eliminate the miracles, angels, and evil spirits, and clean up some of the supernatural gibberish, then you start to have something folks today can relate to.

- **LIKABLE: Jesus is a nice guy.** There are parts of Jesus' message that are indeed appealing—his emphasis on peace, kindness, dignity, justice, freedom, etc. He is certainly one of the greatest moral teachers that ever lived. It's the "Son of God," "forgiveness of sins," and "final judgment" business that seems unnecessary and irrelevant to his cause.

- **LUNATIC: Jesus didn't say what he meant.** Some people during Jesus' lifetime—including family and friends—thought he had clearly gone off the deep end. Maybe he had. The question isn't whether Jesus was sincere. But was he misguided, out of touch, or at times excessively full of himself?

- **LIAR: Jesus didn't mean what he said.** When people lie long enough to themselves, they start lying to others. Is it possible that Jesus intentionally misrepresented the truth and led people astray? Another option here, held widely among Muslims, is that Jesus' followers are the ones responsible for corrupting the texts and handing on misinformation about what Jesus really said and did.

- **LORD: Jesus is what he said, said what he meant, and meant what he said.** We will never be finished studying the texts and seeking deeper understanding of

> *If Jesus is nonexistent, unworthy, inaccessible, or unreliable in any way, then most of what's written in this chapter doesn't really matter.*

Jesus' life, words, and deeds, but what we have and know about Jesus is substantially clear enough that we need to deal with it.

In many ways it comes down to something as simple as this: If Jesus is nonexistent, unworthy, inaccessible, or unreliable in any way, then most of what's written in this chapter doesn't really matter. If, on the other hand, Jesus *is* who he claims to be, then this might just be—in our lives and in the world—the ONLY thing that really matters.

4.

TEACHING, PREACHING, AND HEALING:
What if Jesus' followers did it Jesus' way?

Several years ago I was asked to speak at two commencement ceremonies in different parts of the country, one on the East Coast of the United States and the other in the Midwest. In preparation for these addresses, I conducted informal surveys among the graduating seniors, asking them to identify what they believed would be their greatest challenges as they faced the 21st century.

We live in a messed-up, broken-down world

Not surprisingly, the challenges highlighted were almost as numerous and varied as the students themselves. They ranged from world poverty, societal trends (divorce, suicide), and distressing diseases (like AIDS) to growing materialism, family crises, and the quest for personal happiness and fulfillment.

These students had it right. The issues they were to face would be both global and local, societal as well as personal. There is, in fact, *no part* of the human condition that remains untouched by the profound sense of brokenness permeating our world at every level.

This is no piddly problem we've got on our hands. For, brokenness, as it turns out, is a universal phenomenon. It is comprehensive in nature and scope. And it runs deep—far, far back and beyond our current reality into the near-mythical past of the human experience.

Brokenness runs deep. Many cultures of the world have stories of a Paradise Lost within their collective memory—an original state of harmony and bliss disturbed and destroyed when something went drastically wrong. These stories take us back in time, back beyond the actual memory of clan historians, back to the earliest days of human origins when, out of deceit, arrogance, jealousy, or some other kind of disruptive or disobedient behavior, brokenness entered the world and changed the human story forever.

Though these ancient accounts vary greatly in detail, they share this lesson in common: The world has been living in brokenness for a mighty long time—so long, in fact, that we can't even imagine what our existence would be like without it. Brokenness runs deep. It's a fact of life. It's the way things are. And, for all practical purposes, it's the way they've always been.

Brokenness runs deep. It's a fact of life. It's the way things are. And, for all practical purposes, it's the way they've always been.

> *Ever notice how the word "peace" keeps cropping up in so many of the places where God's big, cosmic plan is the subject of conversation?*

Brokenness is universal. The specific shape of brokenness is determined in part by the culture or society in which it finds expression. In some cultural contexts, this translates into alienation or loss of meaning in life. In other settings, it takes the form of materialistic obsession, political oppression, or evil spirit possession. Whatever the particulars of brokenness in any given place and among any people, it is clear that no culture or society can claim immunity to the problem. For in every human setting, there are those who lie and deceive. Those who take things belonging to someone else. Those who cheat on their spouses. Who beat their children. And treat others in ways that defy all sense of human dignity.

Brokenness is comprehensive. The problem is not only deep within the human past; it is deep within the human being. And no part of that being—body, soul, or mind—has emerged unscathed from the effects of this devastating blow. Healing is needed all around—healing that alone can bring peace of mind, soundness of body, and joy to the heart.

For such a very big problem, an equally big solution is required

The Bible makes it clear that God is fully aware of our sad state of affairs. And it is for this precise reason that God has devised a plan—a plan to come to our rescue, to heal our brokenness, to bring peace out of conflict, and to make things right, once and for all, with the world.

Jesus is at the very heart of God's plan. "For it was *through the Son,*" writes the apostle Paul, "that God decided to bring the whole universe back to himself. God made peace through his Son's death on the cross and so brought back to himself all things, both on earth and in heaven" (Colossians 1:20).

Ever notice how the word "peace" keeps cropping up in so many of the places where God's big, cosmic plan is the subject of conversation? Strange? Not really. For it is precisely this word "peace" that is used over and over again throughout holy history to describe what God is up to in the world. Everywhere we turn, it seems, we run into "peace."

- **The Old Testament prophesied it:** God's suffering servant would be called the Prince of *Peace.*

- **The angel choir proclaimed it:** *Peace* on earth! A Savior is born!

- **Jesus himself pronounced it:** The blessed ones are those working for *peace.*

- **The first Christians preached it:** In Christ, we have *peace* with God and with each other.

But isn't "peace," too small a word to carry all the weight of dismantling the heavy burden of brokenness and setting things right with the world? If we limit ourselves to the English-language term "peace," it probably is. But behind this term is another word. A Hebrew word. The word is *shalom.*

The noun *shalom* occurs some 235 times in the Old Testament and more than 100 times in its Greek translation, *eirene,* in the New Testament. *Shalom* is a very broad concept. That's a good thing, since, as we've already noted, we are indeed faced with a very broad dilemma.

SHALOM *is a broad concept, essential to the Hebrew understanding of relation between people and God. It covers human welfare, health, and well-being in both spiritual and material aspects. It describes a condition of well-being resulting from sound relationships among people and between people and God . . .*

For the Hebrews, peace was not merely the absence of armed conflict. Rather, shalom was assured by the prevalence of conditions which contribute to human well-being in all its dimensions. Not mere tranquility of spirit or serenity of mind, peace had to do with harmonious relationships between God and His people. It had to do with social relationships characterized by His people. It had to do with social relationships characterized by justice.

Peace resulted when people lived together according to God's intentions. Peace, justice, and salvation are synonymous terms for general well-being created by right social relationships.

John Driver, *Community and Commitment* (Scottdale, Pa.: Herald Press, 1976), p. 71.

There is no single word in English that captures the full meaning of the Hebrew word *shalom*. Perry Yoder, in his 1987 book on this matter, alerts us to the term's complexity in the very title he chose for his work, *Shalom: The Bible's Word for Salvation, Justice and Peace.*

Salvation, justice, and peace. That's already about as much as we can handle. But there's more. In other biblical passages, the term is also used to describe a state of health, righteousness, well-being, security, wholeness, integrity, abundance, intactness, honesty, prosperity, right relationships, protection, life-giving-ness, harmony, straightforwardness, reconciliation, blamelessness, rightness, and good accord.

Sometimes in the biblical text these terms appear to be covering a wide range of unrelated realities. Sometimes they seem to be used differently in their Old and New Testament contexts. But, in general, there is a clear sense of continuity and connectedness between these words, permitting us to assert the following about them:

1. **These words are central to God's big project.** God has stepped forward and provided a comprehensive response to a comprehensive problem. When brokenness and sin are experienced at every level of the human experience, then peace, healing, salvation, and wholeness must be equally present at all levels as well. And that is precisely what God's multi-dimensional *shalom*-making project intends to offer.

2. **These words are about relationships.** *Shalom* addresses the problem of broken relationships in whatever form they come—relationships between people, between people and nature, between people and God. "*All things* in heaven and earth will be brought together in Christ," says Paul. And so "all things" it shall

be. All things personal and social. Physical and spiritual. Emotional and ecological. Wherever broken relationships can be found—inward, outward, or upward—healing help and hope are on the way.

3. **These words belong together.** To get the full picture of God's *shalom*-making plan, many and varied descriptive words define it. These words are closely interrelated, "all branches growing from a single tree," as biblical scholar Ulrich Mauser puts it. Each of the terms adds needed color and meaning to our understanding of what God is up to in the world. Keeping the terms together means, among other things, that we cannot strive for prosperity at the expense of justice. Nor can we acquire abundance while losing our integrity. Or seek security and sacrifice peace. God's gift of *shalom* does not come to us as a smorgasbord of selectable options. It is a whole-package offer, all wrapped up into one.

4. **These words depict the way things ought to be.** God's *shalom* is not simply the absence of armed conflict. It is an all-encompassing vision of the way things ought to be at every level of our existence if and when God's will and ways are fully embraced and faithfully practiced. *Shalom* is not a negative concept, but a posi-

---

If Jesus really is the one God has designated as the primary Shalom-Maker, then it should not surprise us to discover in his life and ministry the clearest picture we will ever get of God's big project.

tive one. It is a plan for the transformation of human life and relationships under God's leadership where "old things are passing away" and "all things are becoming new."

5. **These words describe Jesus' life and ministry.** If Jesus really is the one God has designated as the primary *Shalom*-Maker, then it should not surprise us to discover in his life and ministry the clearest picture we will ever get of God's big project. "We look at the Son and see the God who cannot be seen," writes Paul to the believers in Colossae. "We look at the Son and see God's original purpose in everything created" (Colossians 1:15, adapted from Eugene Peterson's, *The Message*).

"Teaching, preaching, and healing"— Jesus' way of keeping God's act together

Maybe the time has come for us to spend less time wondering "What *would* Jesus do?" and more time examining what he actually *did* do. Jesus did a lot of things, that's clear. Four Gospel-books full. Even then, what we find there is apparently only a fraction of the story. At the end of John's account of Jesus' life and ministry, the evangelist openly and almost proudly declares, "Jesus did many other things as well. If every one of them were written down, I suppose that even the whole world would not have room for the books that would be written" (21:25).

What we already possess, however, is largely sufficient to paint a rich tableau for us of what God's *shalom* project looks like when it comes to us in human form, when it walks our streets, eats our food, and confronts the problems and challenges of our world. It is here that we come closest to understanding God's desire for all humanity—

when we follow along after Jesus, accompanying him on his journey through the towns and villages of his homeland, watching him enter broken lives, offering forgiveness, new beginnings, healing, and wholeness to all he meets along the way.

Nearly 20 centuries separate us from Jesus' life and times. Yet much of the brokenness present in his day can be found equally in our world as well. Then, as now, we encounter:

- physical infirmity
- social inequality
- religious hypocrisy
- economic disparity
- racial partiality
- cultural hegemony
- intellectual inadequacy
- political tyranny
- ethnic superiority
- emotional instability
- spiritual captivity

And then, as now, Jesus comes into the human situation, encounters and confronts people of all stripes and standings in their areas of deepest need, and invites them to embrace God's liberating, saving grace in their lives.

Jesus knew exactly what part of *shalom* the self-righteousness Pharisees needed to hear, and he delivered it to them with great gusto. He also knew what *shalom* might look like for blind Bartimaeus, for curious Nicodemus, for cheating Zacchaeus, for the adulterous woman, the repentant criminal, the self-sufficient rich man, the anxious poor folk, and the starving masses.

In many instances, Jesus began with the most obvious, presenting need before him, and then took people to a level they had never anticipated going. "You think you have done all that is necessary to obey the law? Go, sell your possessions and give to the poor" (rich man). "Thanks for the drink of water from your well. But I can give you living water so you will never be thirsty again" (Samaritan woman). "Congratulations for having recognized me as God's anointed one, the Messiah. Now, let me tell you how the Messiah will need to suffer and die" (Peter). "Your sins are forgiven. Go, then, and sin no more" (adulterous woman). "Okay, so we've fed the hungry crowds with loaves of bread. Be careful. Don't work for food that spoils, but for food that endures. I am the bread of life. If you come to me, you will never go hungry again" (the disciples).

When Jesus goes around spreading God's *shalom*, all of the pieces of God's big project come through in a seamless kind of way. It's not as if Jesus gets up one morning and says, "Okay, today will be 'Justice Day.' Gotta talk about that all day long. And, let's see, how about making tomorrow 'Peace Day.' And then Wednesday, we'll do 'Health Day,' followed by 'Wholeness Day,' 'Salvation Day,' and so on, until we make the rounds."

The gospel writer Matthew sums up Jesus' ministry this way: "And Jesus went through all the towns and villages, *teaching* in their synagogues, *preaching* the good news of the kingdom and *healing* every kind of disease and sickness" (9:35). Teaching, preaching, and healing, Matthew

In many instances, Jesus began with the most obvious, presenting need before him, and then took people to a level they had never anticipated going.

> *Somehow, over the years, the church preferred*
> *to have* shalom *chopped up in fragmented bits*
> *and pieces rather than embracing it as an inte-*
> *grated whole.*

says. How holistic is that? Stimulating people's minds to think clearly about God's work in the world. Challenging their hearts to experience God's goodness in new and transforming ways. And ministering to their bodies so that they can be everything God created them to be.

So why is the church still fighting over ghosts and corpses?

The story is told of two small-town churches which for years waged a war of words over the true nature of the gospel.

The conflict first erupted when one of the churches posted boldly on its marquee: "We preach the Word so that souls might be saved." Within days, the church across the street responded: "The Word can't be heard when the stomach growls with hunger."

"He who eats of the Bread of Life will hunger no more," came the quick reply. Only to be countered with: "I was hungry and you gave me nothing to eat. Go, then, to the place of eternal punishment!"

The most creative exchange occurred when the first church declared, "The body without a soul is but a corpse," followed immediately with, "The soul without a body is a ghost."

This story wouldn't be so sadly funny if it weren't so true. Which of these congregations had it right? Well, both, of course. And neither. Somehow, over the years, the church preferred to have *shalom* chopped up in fragmented bits and pieces rather than embracing it as an integrated whole. And so we have created Evangelism Committees, Service Committees, Peace and Justice Committees, Environmental Care Committees, Health and Welfare Committees, and as many more committees as we deem necessary for carrying out God's work in the world.

Unfortunately, many of the people on these various committees never speak to each other. Some of them downright wouldn't want to. Others simply see no need for it. "We're just not on the same page," is the reason they give for their separate agenda.

It's not clear to me, however, when we carve things up in this manner, what page we think we're on. One thing is certain: We're *not* on the page that has as its main title and principal theme, "God's Shalom Project as Seen in Jesus."

Suppose we gave the Lord of Creation another chance?

In the spring of 1980, Jeanette and I were auditing courses at the Catholic Institute of West Africa in Abidjan, Ivory Coast. One day we arrived for classes at the institute and were greeted with some truly incredible news: The Pope was coming to town!

First, people were stunned. Then there was a flurry of frantic activity as the entire campus mobilized to prepare for his arrival. Lawns were mowed, bushes trimmed, windows washed, floors scrubbed—all in an attempt to make ready for the first African voyage of the one who would eventually become known as the "traveling pontiff," John Paul II.

The highlight of the week-long celebration for the 80-some students and faculty members at the institute was when the teeming throngs of pilgrims and onlookers were held at bay for two hours outside the campus premises while the pope conducted an informal "pastoral conversation" with the professors and students inside.

As a general rule in Ivory Coast, one can always find perfectly good and legitimate reasons for tardiness or for the need to cancel fixed appointments due to sudden illness, transportation breakdowns, deaths in the family, and so on. But, believe me, on *this* day, not a single invited guest showed up missing! The dead buried the dead. Broken-down buses sprouted wings. And the sick picked up their beds and walked. Nothing next to *nothing* could have prevented participants from being present at this once-in-a-lifetime experience.

Now, suppose, just suppose, someone *else* was coming to town, someone a tad more important than the pope, someone like . . . God-In-Human-Form. How much might one expect to scrub the floors or rearrange one's schedule for *that* encounter? Or, what if the person arriving were, The-One-Who-Existed-Before-All-Things, The-One-By-Whom-And-Through-Whom-All-Things-Were-Created, or The-One-Of-Whom-All-The-Prophets-Have-Spoken? How special would it be to be selected for a private audience with a personage of this stature?

If it is true that Jesus stands at the very center of human history, dividing the story of the world into "before" and "after," then it makes perfect sense that we might want to find out as much about him as possible. And if it is true that by looking at Jesus we can learn more about God than through any other means, then paying close attention to what he actually said and did during his life on earth would appear to be an activity well worth our time and energy.

It was, of course, the firm conviction of the first-century faith community that Jesus—the Lord of Creation—had,

> *If it is true that Jesus stands at the very center of human history, dividing the story of the world into "before" and "after," then it makes perfect sense that we might want to find out as much about him as possible.*

in fact, come to town. "The Word became a human being and lived among us," says the gospel writer John (1:14). Eugene Peterson's *The Message* puts it like this: "The Word became flesh and blood, and moved into the neighborhood." Either way, we're talking about an up-close-and-personal human encounter. "We have seen his glory," continues John, "the glory of the one and only coming from the Father, full of grace and truth."

Jane Vonnegut Yarmolinsky, in Lauren Winner's book, *Girl Meets God,* is quoted as saying, "For people with bodies, simple things like love have to be embodied . . . God had to be embodied, or else people with bodies would never in a trillion years understand about love."

Jesus comes to us as the one who embodies God's love. But he also embodies God's justice, God's righteousness, God's peace and salvation . . . he embodies, in short, God's *shalom*. This is what we have *seen* in Jesus—to use John's expression—though how this could or should affect our lives remains for each of us a wide-open question.

To look into the caring, compassionate face of Jesus and outright disavow his role as God's *Shalom*-Maker in the world is probably more mean-spirited than most of us would wish or choose to be. To acknowledge, on the other hand, this role for Jesus and to begin entertaining thoughts of what this might ultimately mean has enormous potential for turning our lives upside down. For it most surely won't be long until some of the "old things" we've believed or done "will begin passing away," and in their place will be the invigorating, life-altering challenge of redefining and reshaping virtually every relationship we've ever had—with our natural environment, with our innermost selves, with our neighbors, both friends and enemies . . . and with our God.

5.

THE CHURCH:
Until further notice, there's no back-up plan

Most people are pretty picky about what church they choose to attend. The worship needs to be decent. The facility clean, attractive, and welcoming. The children's program up-to-snuff. The pastor friendly, upright, good-looking, articulate, caring, athletic, intelligent, ever-available . . . all the things a good pastor needs to be. And in addition to these things, it's nice to be associated with a congregation that is highly visible and well thought of in the town or community where it is located.

So imagine rolling out of bed some Saturday morning

From the moment I knocked on the church door at HHCF and was greeted by four individuals, all claiming to be the "senior pastor," I knew I was in trouble.

and opening up the Religion section of your local newspaper to find the following special front-page feature on Healing and Hope Community Fellowship—the congregation you happen to be presently attending.

Healing and Hope Community Fellowship Faces Multiple Crises

Following up on a tip from one of the church members at Healing and Hope Community Fellowship, our reporter, Rhea Lystik, made a special visit this week to HHCF to investigate whether the rumors of alleged chaos at the church were as serious as reported. Here is what she found:

HOMETOWN, U.S.A.—From the moment I knocked on the church door at HHCF and was greeted by four individuals, all claiming to be the "senior pastor," I knew I was in trouble. How do you conduct an interview when you've got four people expecting to have the final word on every subject?

We tried the group interview approach for a while, but it was a disaster. These characters were not in the least bit bothered or embarrassed about walking and talking all over each other to make sure I heard their personal point of view. One fellow—who introduced himself as "Reverend So-and-So, Bachelor of Arts, Master of Divinity, Doctor of Philosophy in Deuteronominalistical . . . (gasp) . . .", almost dying of oxygen loss before eking out his nth degree—proceeded to present himself lexicographically in what I later discovered to be an entire page of text lifted directly from *Roget's Thesaurus of English Words and Phrases.* A second figure—jokingly dubbed The Flapper by his fellow colleagues-in-ministry—eventually cut off Reverend So-

and-So, and weaseled his way into the spotlight by erupting forth in some kind of high-spirited, Christianese gibberish that only angels could have possibly been equipped to understand.

I determined to bring the group back down to earth and try to find some common ground by asking to see the church membership directory. There wasn't "one," I was informed. There were . . . four, one for each of the pastors who kept separate lists of members baptized "under their charge."

"So . . . how are things going *otherwise* at HHCF?" I asked, reaching for some sense of the broader congregational profile beyond the intense personal squabbles clearly present among members of the pastoral leadership team. "Oh, we've got a pretty off-the-wall bunch of people around here," came the immediate response. (I'll have to admit that didn't surprise me in the least.)

"There's one guy in the congregation," said Reverend So-and-So, "who's just moved in with his stepmother. Some people think that's kinda sleazy and accuse them of shacking up together. I personally think it's a little rude and insensitive to talk about these folks that way. As long as the two of them really love each other and nobody's getting hurt, I don't see why people have to get so upset.

"And then we've got two young couples clawing each others' eyes out in the courts over some property issues. That occasionally makes for some rather tense moments on Sunday morning during the coffee break between Sunday school hour and the worship service. But most of the time people manage to leave their private affairs at home rather than dragging all that stuff into church and disturbing the rest of us with it.

"And, oh yes, we *do* have a handful of party animals here at HHCF who just never seem to calm down. At last month's potluck we ended the evening with a Love Feast celebrating the Lord's Supper as a congregation. Unfortunately, a few members got a little carried away with the 'blood of Christ' and ended up smashed out of their skulls. The Hostess Committee has since decided that the church will need to either start providing a shuttle service or designating safe drivers if we're going to accommodate all the diversity we've got here in the congregation."

I had had about enough of HHCF for one day and began packing my stuff to leave. I met The Flapper on the way out. "Hey!" he bubbled. "Make sure you come back on Sunday. Guess who's leading worship? I am! It's gonna be a hoppin' hoot! People get crazy when The Flapper's in charge! You never know *what's* gonna happen!"

"I'll bet you don't," I said, heading out the door.

Front side or back side, you end up with the same data

If I have just described the life and leadership of your congregation, please accept my sincerest apologies. It was in no way intentional. What was intentional was the desire to place in a 21st-century context a few of the real-life crises faced by an actual first-century congregation—the church in the city of Corinth—presented to us in the pages of the New Testament.

Just to put things in perspective, I was actually being kind to Corinth in my news feature reconstruction above. For in addition to the issues of leadership conflict, questionable sexual behavior, gluttony, substance abuse, religious frenzy, and spiritual elitism, the congregation also struggled with various forms of idolatry and paganized feasts, superstition, demonism, magic, philosophical skepticism, heretical teaching, materialism, gender issues, and social strife. Let's just say that the four "senior pastors"—when they were not actually creating *more* problems for the church—had their hands full.

In reviewing again the almost insurmountable challenges faced by the church in Corinth, I was reminded of an informal survey I conducted several years ago in a mostly rural, northern Indiana congregation. Invited there to speak on the topic, "The Whole Gospel of Jesus for a Broken World," I distributed blank sheets of paper to those attending and asked them to list all the forms of brokenness they could think of that characterized the society in which they lived.

The results were not particularly surprising—divorce scored highest on the roster, followed by intergenerational conflict, drugs, infidelity, and about a dozen other items one might expect to find on a list of this nature. Then I asked the participants to write down on the back side of the sheet the principal forms of brokenness they were experiencing in their own personal lives and in the life of their congregation. This second list came back almost identical to the first: divorce, intergenerational conflict, drugs, infidelity, etc.—prompting, as one might have anticipated, a number of interesting and understandable reactions from people in the congregation:

> *Either there's another church in Corinth we don't know about and to whom Paul is writing. Or the apostle is in major denial. Or he is downright crazy.*

- "So, what's the point of being the church if we're no different than the people living around us?"

- "That just goes to show that the church is made up of a bunch of hypocrites who go around acting like they're better than everybody else, when really they're not."

- "Isn't it embarrassing to invite people from outside the church to our congregation when we've got all these problems we're dealing with?"

- "I think we need to just put Missions on hold for awhile and focus on cleaning up our own act first. Maybe then we'll have some good news to share with others."

Excuse me, but would you mind repeating that "holy" part again?

All of this makes the apostle Paul's opening words of greeting even more remarkable when he writes to those back-stabbing, wine-guzzling, stepmother-seducing believers in Corinth. "To the church of God in Corinth," he writes, "to those *sanctified in Christ Jesus and called to be holy . . ."* (1 Corinthians 1:2). What? Wait a minute, are we sure we have the right text here? "To you Christians cleaned up by Jesus and set apart for a God-filled life," as *The Message* puts it. Plain English makes it sound even more unlikely!

What's going on here? Either there's another church in Corinth we don't know about and to whom Paul is writing. Or the apostle is in major denial. Or he is downright crazy. Or . . . he is working off a much larger spreadsheet than most of us do—the spreadsheet of history, of God's big plan to reconcile *all things* in the universe to himself through Jesus Christ.

In this longer view of things, Paul recognizes right from the start that central to the divine initiative is God's desire and intention to reach down and to make something of a bunch of good-for-nothin' rascals. God wants to set them on their feet, and to empower them to join with him in "setting things right with the world." This is, in fact, precisely why, according to Paul, Jesus offered up his own life

How Western Christians saw themselves and other faiths in the 1870 publication, The Natural History of Man, *by the Rev. J. G. Wood.*

> *Most followers of Jesus really don't have a whole lot to go around bragging about.*

on our behalf, "to redeem us from all wickedness and *to purify for himself a people* that are his very own, eager to do what is good" (Titus 2:14).

So, that makes these good-for-nothin' rascals pretty special people all of a sudden, doesn't it? Well, yes and no. At one level, nothing much changes. They remain what they are and always will be—good-for-nothin' rascals. And even if they do manage to become something more than that, it will not be of their own doing, but only because God has been mighty good to them. "For it is by grace you have been saved, through faith—and this not from yourselves, it is the gift of God—not by human effort, so that no one can go around bragging about it" (Ephesians 2:8, 9).

As it turns out, of course, most followers of Jesus really don't have a whole lot to go around bragging about. They are little more than a band of undeserving rascals cleaned up by Jesus for no other reason than that God has loved them and chosen to make them a part of the Grand Plan to "bring everyone and everything together in Christ." This is already in itself very good news. But it's not the end of the story.

What follows is, in my mind, even more amazing. No, it's not just amazing. It's craziness—from a strictly human point of view—bordering on irresponsibility and poor judgment. Never in our wildest dreams as human beings could we have cooked it up as the logical next step in carrying out God's Grand-Plan-For-Reconciling-All-Things-In-The-Entire-Universe. The whole idea is just too fraught with risks, too likely to fail. Even the angels in heaven, as Ron Sider speculates in his introduction to *Genuine Christianity,* are likely left with their mouths hanging wide open at such an outrageous prospect. And what is that prospect? That God might willingly decide to turn around and entrust his Cosmic *Shalom*-Making Project—the world's most precious possession and the only hope for getting the universe back on track—to the very bunch of good-for-nothin' rascals who have been its undeserving recipients.

What was God thinking, anyway?

And yet . . . this is precisely what God has apparently chosen to do. Follow along with Sider as he describes what might have been the reaction of the archangel Gabriel when this bit of incredible news became known in heaven:

> Imagine for a moment this astonishing, imaginary conversation that Jesus might have had with the archangel Gabriel upon his triumphant return to heaven.
>
> "Well, how did it go?" Gabriel asks Jesus. "Did you complete your mission and save the world?"
>
> "Well, yes and no," Jesus replies. "I modeled a godly life for about thirty years. I preached to a few thousand Jews in one corner of the Roman Empire. I died for the sins of the world and promised that those who believe in me will live forever. And I burst from the tomb on the third day to show my circle of 120 frightened followers that my life and story are God's way to save the whole world. Then I gave the Holy Spirit to those 120 and left them to finish the task."
>
> "You mean," Gabriel asks in amazement, "your whole plan to save the world depends on that ragtag bunch of fishermen, ex-prostitutes, and tax collectors?"
>
> "That's right," Jesus replies.
>
> "But what if they fail?" Gabriel persists with growing alarm. "What's your back-up plan?

"There is no back-up plan," Jesus says quietly (Sider, 1996:11).

It is precisely this firm conviction that inspires the apostle Paul to address those sewage-drenched Christians in Corinth as "you who are sanctified in Christ Jesus and called to be holy." It is the same belief that emboldens him to announce to the believers in Ephesus the truly mind-boggling news that—are you ready for this one?—it is *"through the church* that the rulers and authorities in the heavenly realms will learn of God's wisdom in all its different forms" (Ephesians 3:10).

ENTER: The Church—model *and* messenger *of God's Cosmic Project*

God is working on a big Project of setting things right with the world. The Project is not and never has been the *church's* idea; it originates with God and with God alone. Nor does the church in any way own The Project; it belongs only to God who alone sustains it and will bring it to pass. The church has, however, been invited and equipped by God to participate in The Project by serving in two primary ways, as *model* and as *messenger*.

The church as model. You want to know what The Project looks like, asks Paul? Look at the church. Watch how she worships. Listen to her praying. Hear the joyful sounds of her music. Witness how her members treat each other. Notice the many ways she experiences and extends God's grace and forgiveness. See how her life is being constantly transformed. Look how Jesus stands in her midst. Watch how the Spirit pours out gifts to strengthen every part of the community. Listen as she finds the courage to name her shortcomings and call out to God in repentance. Hear the

> *It is precisely this firm conviction that inspires the apostle Paul to address those sewage-drenched Christians in Corinth as "you who are sanctified in Christ Jesus and called to be holy."*

sounds of laughter as people long separated by race, gender, and class become reconciled and form a new family of faith.

The church as messenger. As people experience more and more of God's grace and reconciling power in their lives, the destructive patterns and senseless cycles of the past, asserts Paul, will begin to give way to fresh starts, second chances, and new beginnings—almost as if the world were being created all over again (2 Corinthians 5:17). This tremendous gift from God is not to be limited, however, to some specially-privileged group of people, huddling quietly in a hidden, out-of-the-way corner of the universe. Quite to the contrary, says Paul. God has chosen to make his appeal to the rest of the world through those very ones who have already experienced *shalom* in their own individual lives and in their life together as a community of faith. And that is why, according to Paul, "God has committed to us the message of reconciliation," making us Christ's ambassadors to the world (2 Corinthians 5:19-20).

There is no indication, so far as I'm aware, that God has given us the option of choosing between being either a "model" or a "messenger" of the plan. There are not two separate "callings" here; only one, in two modes. We should know that, in any case, by simply looking at the way Jesus lived *his* life. Was Jesus, as God's primary *Shalom*-Maker in the world, a "model" of The Cosmic Project, or was he its "messenger"? The answer, of course, is . . . *yes!* He was both. In a seamless, indivisible kind of way.

Jesus seems to have known what we should also know: that *preaching* about The Project without *practicing* it has little integrity. And that *practicing* it without *preaching* it leaves people in the dark as to the ultimate source and deeper meaning of one's actions. Both *demonstration* and *explanation* are required for people to fully see and understand what God is up to in the world. Both work *and* witness, word *and* deed, are essential if the full scope of God's love is to be known.

Wake up, Church! Embrace your calling!

There are perhaps no moments in church history more tragic than those when Christians have either intentionally or out of ignorance dissected the gospel, separating parts from each other that really belonged together and producing in the process a diluted, distorted version of the very gospel they were purporting to represent.

Rodney Clapp, in *A Peculiar People,* reminds us of one such case dating back to the 16th-century European conquest of the Latin American continent. The Spanish conquistadors, reports Clapp, called on the Indian population *through their words* to take Jesus as their Savior. Yet *through their actions* they habitually "lied to the Indians, so that when Indians were asked if they were Christians, they quite seriously replied, 'Yes, sir, I am a bit Christian because I have learned to lie a bit; another day I will lie big, and I will be a big Christian.'"

In another incident closer home, I am reminded of a conversation I had in the mid-1990s with my friend Jasper Ndaborlor, a pastor from the West African country of Liberia. At the time of our conversation, Liberia was still in the heat of a five-year-long civil war. Over 50,000 peo-

> Preaching *about The Project without* practicing *it has little integrity. And* practicing *it without* preaching *it leaves people in the dark as to the ultimate source and deeper meaning of one's actions.*

ple had by that time lost their lives, and the widespread problems of hunger, violence, trauma, drug abuse, and homelessness were rapidly bringing the country to a standstill. "Christians make up almost 40 percent of the Liberian population," Jasper told me. "But most Christians 'spiritualize' their faith, thinking of it only as a passport to heaven sometime in the future, in the 'sweet by and by.' So when we were faced with the challenges of ethnic conflict," he said, "most people made no connection between the reconciling nature of the gospel and the tribal clashes erupting all around them." Jasper paused, and then continued with new resolve. "I have come to believe we need a deeper understanding of the gospel," he said. "I am convinced that if Liberian Christians had understood what God's *shalom* was really all about, they alone—as one mighty force—could have prevented this entire devastating war from happening."

God took an enormous risk in choosing us as human beings to be the primary agents for living out and getting out the word about his cosmic reconciliation project. The fact that we have not always done such a fabulous job at the assignment in no way changes the basic strategy God has put in place.

It probably wouldn't hurt us as God's people to spend more time talking about how to live our calling more

> *"I am convinced that if Liberian Christians
> had understood what God's* shalom *was really
> all about, they alone—as one mighty force—
> could have prevented this entire devastating
> war from happening."*

faithfully. Particularly since our past performance hasn't always been too brilliant. And because—despite that rather sobering fact—God has apparently decided not to put an alternative, back-up plan in place.

6.
BIBLE OR
NEWSPAPER:
Feeling the tension is a healthy sign

Bats have got to be some of the most confused critters on the face of the earth. Look at the poor guys. They really don't belong on the ground scurrying about like their rodent cousins. They've got wings, for pity's sakes. So up they go into the air, soaring around like mice with an attitude. Except they really don't seem to belong there either.

It must be difficult making friends if you're a bat. Imagine trying to get chummy with a robin? Nope, you don't fit in. How about moving into the muskrat neighborhood? Not much better there.

There are lots of funny stories about bats in Africa. In Liberia, people say that bats are really two creatures in one. The "b" in bat comes from "bird," because bats have wings and spend so much time flying about. And the "at" in bat comes from "rat," because that's essentially what they are. So there you have it. Bats are really bird-rats, conflicted to the core, living in two worlds and belonging to neither.

One African elder told me once that God had been kind to bats. He made them blind. "Bats have enough problems in life," he chuckled, "without having to look in the mirror." And so what do these confused creatures do? They grab hold of the nearest limb and hang themselves—upside down, that is—not with the intention of ending it all, but in a position that makes it very difficult for them not to increase their misery by pooping on themselves.

My life as a bat

I have sometimes felt like a bat. I felt like one in my very first year of school when my kindergarten teacher, whom I shall call, Mrs. Humphreys, forced me into a showdown in front of the entire class. One of my classmates—I'll call him Billy, though "bully" better fits my recollection—had picked a fight with me, hitting me in the face, and then shoving me in the back when I chose to walk away. Sensing a teachable moment in the making, Mrs. Humphreys gathered all the other students together in a circle around us and announced, "James and Billy need to learn some lessons here today. Billy needs to know that he can't just go around clobbering people without consequences. And James needs to learn not to just walk away from people who are doing him wrong."

"And so, James," she continued, looking me straight in the eyes, "Billy has been unfairly pushing you around here this morning and now I want you to hit him back so we can all see what to do if this kind of thing should *ever* happen again." Time stood still. I refused. She insisted. I balked. She fumed. I struck. But I remember feeling more like a bat than a boy that day, conflicted by the inner tension of my conscience and the rules of kindergarten con-

> *We could not for the life of us understand, during those days of bicentennial fervor, why so many of our compatriots were convinced you either had to "love America, or leave it."*

duct that Mrs. Humphreys was establishing as standard classroom behavior.

I have felt like a bat at various other times in my life, as well. One of those came in 1976 when America was celebrating her 200th birthday. My wife, Jeanette, and I were preparing that summer to leave for a two-year term of international service, first in France for language study, and then on to Ivory Coast for a teaching assignment with a West African church movement there.

We were working very hard to readjust our cultural lenses, to understand what life might look like from another's point of view. And we were growing in our awareness of what God was doing around the world in breaking down age-old barriers and bringing together a new family of faith, assembled from every tribe and nation. We could not for the life of us understand, during those days of bicentennial fervor, why so many of our compatriots were convinced you either had to *"love* America, or *leave* it." Were those really our *only* options, we wondered? "The love of one's country," wrote Pablo Casals, "is a splendid thing. But why should love stop at the border?" Now *that's* the kind of question we thought more people should be asking.

There were moments in 1976 when we thought for sure we were going, well . . . *batty*, which, of course, we were.

And things over the years tended only to get worse. Navigating back and forth for two decades from America to France, England, and Africa did little to assure us that we'd ever find a true place to belong. On one return trip to Ivory Coast, following a three-month stint in the States, I overheard our six-year old son, Matthew, explain to one of his close friends, "We just go back and forth—America, Africa; America, Africa; America, Africa—until we get dizzy, and then we don't know where we are."

Followers of Jesus should understand perfectly well the bat's dilemma

From the earliest years of the Christian movement and continuing right up until the present time, the followers of Jesus have found themselves living between two worlds— the world where God's Cosmic Reconciliation Project reigns supreme and the more familiar day-to-day world of human reality where that project is being practiced and preached in earth-bound time and space.

We are, of course, not the first ones to find ourselves in a place of tension between these two worlds. Already as early as the mid-second century after Christ, in a remarkable document called the *Letter to Diognetus,* we learn about life in the early Christian movement through the eyes of an apparent outsider and get a peek into how Christians were grappling with this very issue:

> Christians cannot be distinguished from other people by country, language or customs; you see, they do not live in cities of their own, or speak some strange dialect, or have some peculiar lifestyle. . . . They live in both Greek and foreign cities . . . but at the same time, they demonstrate to us the wonderful and certainly unusual form of their own citizenship.

They live in their own native lands, but as resident aliens. . . . Every foreign country is to them as their native country, and every native land as a foreign country.

They marry and have children just like everyone else; but they do not kill unwanted babies. They offer a shared table, but not a shared bed. They are at present "in the flesh" but they do not live "according to the flesh." They are passing their days on earth, but are citizens of heaven. . . . Christians are in the world but not of the world.

Life between the Bible and the newspaper

Charles Spurgeon, a dynamic preacher and prolific author of the late 19th century, wrote a book in 1879 entitled, *The Bible and the Newspaper.* In it he challenged church leaders to become regular readers of the newspaper in order to learn about the life and times in which they lived. Building on a statement by John Newton, Spurgeon wrote: "I read the newspaper that I may see how my heavenly Father governs the world."

Karl Barth, John Stott, and other Christian writers since then have taken Spurgeon's appeal to another level by declaring that any person who truly wishes to be a responsible Christian in today's world must "firmly grasp the Bible in one hand and the newspaper in the other." It is only in holding fast to *both* documents, the argument goes, that

Any person who truly wishes to be a responsible Christian in today's world must "firmly grasp the Bible in one hand and the newspaper in the other."

> *There is nothing Christians like to do more than huddle by themselves off in a corner.*

one can see the vast stage upon which the dramatic story of God's love and faithfulness is being played out.

Holding the Bible in one hand. It is in the Bible that we become best acquainted with God's grand plan to set things right with the world. It is here that we have laid out before us the various chapters and phases of that plan throughout "holy history." And it is in these pages, as well, that we meet Jesus, God's principal *Shalom*-Maker, the One who because of his willingness to "become obedient unto death" has now been "exalted to the highest place and given the name that is above every name . . . in heaven and on earth and under the earth" (Philippians 2:8-10).

Holding the newspaper in the other. The newspaper, on the other hand, serves equally as essential reading for understanding what God is up to in the world. For it is here that we become most keenly aware of the deep and devastating brokenness in our world. It is here that we encounter the issues God's Project must address if it is truly to be received and understood as good news. And it is here, as well, that we get the clearest picture of those people, trends, and movements which are likely to be most threatened and resistant to God's peace-making initiatives in Jesus.

So there you have it. Both documents are necessary reading for those choosing to participate in God's grand plan. One of the documents provides us with the language of faith and the other with the language of our culture. One represents the Word and the other, the world. One is the text and the other, the context. One tells us the news, and the other offers us . . . the *good* news.

Bailing out or caving in—either one by itself and we're "slip slidin' away"

It is no easy task living in that tense spot between the Word and the world, between the news and the good news. It is safer, simpler, and generally less stressful to let oneself slip, and eventually slide, to one side or the other. Whenever that happens, however, God's people get themselves in a heap of trouble.

The problem with "bailing out." One of the greatest temptations for the church is to turn its back on the world and head out to the desert, the countryside, the mountaintop—*anywhere* quiet, cozy, and comfortably distant from the noise and turmoil which make reading the Bible such difficult work.

There is nothing Christians like to do more than huddle by themselves off in a corner. And they find a million ways to do it. They huddle in their church buildings, in their private schools, in their personal friendships, in their contemporary worship music, in their religious language. They even manage to huddle in their evangelistic meetings—meetings which, one would think, might be designed for building bridges to those outside the community of faith but often end up doing little more than nurturing the saints.

The Sunday school movement was first initiated in some communities as a means of attracting and connecting with the specific neighborhood in which a given congregation happened to find itself. With time, however, the educational interests and needs of the congregation's own children began to take precedence over any other considerations—that's the huddling factor!—until finally the original vision for the Sunday school was lost altogether.

Summer Vacation Bible School programs were then introduced in some instances as attempts to rekindle the ear-

Suggested Exercise: Gospel and Culture

Separate all the items that follow into two categories, based on these definitions:

Essential. These items (commands, practices, customs) are essential to the church in every age. (Mark these E on the list.)
Negotiable. These items (commands, practices, customs) may or may not be valid for the church in any given place or time. (Mark these N on the list.)

1. Greet each other with a holy kiss.
2. Do not go to court to settle issues between Christians.
3. Do not eat meat used in pagan ceremonies.
4. Women in the assembly should be veiled when praying or speaking.
5. Wash feet at the Lord's Supper (Eucharist).
6. Lay on hands for ordination.
7. Sing without musical accompaniment.
8. Abstain from eating blood.
9. Abstain from fornication.
10. Share the Lord's Supper (Eucharist) together.
11. Use only real wine and unleavened bread for your Eucharist meals.
12. Use only grape juice for Eucharist meals.
13. Anoint with oil for healing.
14. Women are not to teach men.
15. Women are not to wear braided hair, gold, or pearls.
16. Men are not to have long hair.

17. Do not drink wine at all.

18. Slavery is permissible if you treat slaves well.

19. Remain single.

20. Seek the gift of tongues.

21. Seek the gift of healing.

22. Lift your hands when you pray.

23. People who don't work don't eat.

24. Have a private "devotional time" every day.

25. Say *Amen* at the end of prayers.

26. Appoint elders and deacons in every congregation.

27. Elect the leaders.

28. Confess sins one to another.

29. Confess sins privately to God.

30. Give at least ten per cent of your income/goods/crops to God.

31. Construct a building for worship.

32. Confess Christ publically by means of baptism.

33. Be baptized by immersion.

34. Be baptized as an adult.

35. Be baptized as a child/infant.

36. Do not be a polygamist.

37. Do not divorce your spouse for any reason.

38. Do not divorce your spouse except for adultery.

"The Temporary Gospel," *The Other Side Magazine.* Nov.-Dec. 1975. Copyrighted by and reprinted with permission from *The Other Side Magazine.*

lier fire for local connections. But many of these, too, underwent transformation when the congregation became its own best client—huddling strikes again!—and neighborhood relationships gradually dried up and faded away.

The church has occasionally ventured out from behind its double-bolted doors just long enough to read the headlines in the newspaper. A scary experience . . . although it certainly did provide plenty of food to chew on when church members huddled again at the next mid-week potluck dinner to process the frightening things they had seen out there in the big, bad world.

I've heard a song on Christian radio that echoes the very situation I have just described. The song is called, "Build an Ark," and the chorus goes like this:

> Build an ark;
> Head for the open waters;
> Save your sons and your daughters;
> Build an ark.
> One day when the storm has ended,
> You know the world has been mended,
> Build an ark.

The song's two verses go on to offer the image of Noah's ark as the only safe place to find shelter from a world clearly headed down the tubes:

Verse 1:
> I'm tired of all the villains;
> I'm tired of all the killins';
> I'm tired of all the men who make the laws
> And break them anytime they please.
> I'm tired of all the big lies.
> Where are all the good guys?
> Sometimes I think I feel the way that Noah did
> When the Lord commanded:
> "Build an ark!"

Verse 2:
My father and my mother,
My sisters and my brothers,
All the friends I care about,
And the woman that I learned to love,
I'll gather them together
And promise them forever,
We'll be safe from the world around us.
All we have to do is love each other.
Build an ark!

The main problem with this kind of counsel, of course, is how foreign it sounds when placed alongside the words of Jesus, God's primary *Shalom*-Maker in the world. "I am sending you out like sheep to a pack of wolves," Jesus told his disciples. "If they persecuted me, they'll persecute you, too."

There is no suggestion anywhere in Jesus' teachings, or in those of the early church, that safety and security are a guaranteed part of the deal. No, that is the language of those who have bailed out and are in desperate need of being brought back to that place of risk . . . between the Bible and the newspaper.

The problem with "caving in." Most people eventually get tired of being isolated, or weird, or strung up and killed. And so they start taking a new look at the world in

> *There is no suggestion anywhere in Jesus' teachings, or in those of the early church, that safety and security are a guaranteed part of the deal.*

> *Christians who seriously read not only the Bible, but also the newspaper, will find themselves endlessly drawn into the process of translating God's eternal Word into the language of their ever-changing world.*

which they live. The Bible *does* tell us, after all, to become all things to all people, they begin to reason. And so, tucking this mandate firmly under their arms, they proceed to do just that.

I distinctly remember the exhilaration of the 1960s when my own church began to emerge from a long period of relative isolationism into increased awareness of and more active engagement with "the world." This was a significant enough cultural shift that we adopted a whole new vocabulary for describing what was happening to us. Suddenly, we were "in," we were cool, we were hip, but mostly we were. . . relevant. *That* was the qualifier that somehow felt the most gratifying.

Being relevant came to us in all forms—paraphrasing the Scriptures into contemporary discourse, exchanging the boring black leather covers on our Bibles for down-home denim, and timidly introducing folk and light rock music into our churches' worship experiences. (This was the closest that some of us have ever come to being strung up and killed.)

I remember visiting a friend of mine during this period who had posted a plaque on his bedroom wall asking the question, "What is Jesus like?" The answers followed, "Jesus is like Coke; he's the *real* thing!" "Jesus is like General Electric; he lights up your path!" "Jesus is like Tide; he gets the stains out that others leave behind!" "Jesus is like Scotch tape; you can't see him but you know he's there!" How cool was that, I thought, to use taglines from well-known commercials to freshen up the totally stale formulations we were getting on Sunday mornings and in other churchified settings.

The fact is, Christians who seriously read not only the Bible, but also the newspaper, will find themselves endlessly drawn into the process of translating God's eternal Word into the language of their ever-changing world.

Problems arise, however, when Christians choose to read *only* the newspaper. When that happens, it is never long until one sees them first sucking up, then selling out, and finally "slip slidin' away" from that central point of tension to which they are called. "He who sups with the devil had better have a long spoon," writes Peter Berger in *A Rumor of Angels*. Berger's warning concerned modernity, but the same could be equally applied to the church's fascination with relevancy. "The devilry of [relevancy] has its own magic. The [Christian] who sups with it will find his spoon getting shorter and shorter—until that last supper in which he is left alone at the table, with no spoon at all and with an empty plate."

When this happens, the Church becomes so relevant she becomes irrelevant, and her message of Good News is reduced to little more than . . . news.

Living in the middle with the tension isn't all that . . . bat!

Fortunately, dysfunctional dizziness—or, in bat behavior, hanging upside down and pooping on oneself—is not life's only option. A turning point for me along this journey came with an article I read in the mid-1980s by the Senegalese author-politician Leopold Senghor, entitled, *"L'avenir appar-*

tient aux métisses" (or, "the future belongs to those of mixed origins—the mulattos"). Senghor was well placed to understand this reality. Black West-African in origin, and married to a white French woman, he and his wife were the parents of children whom he described as *"à cheval entre deux races et cultures"* ("straddling, like a horse-back rider, two races and cultures").

As he observed his own children and reflected on the worlds in which they lived, he came to admire and even envy their natural, intuitive capacity to commute freely between diverse realities. Far from a *curse*, said Senghor, being bi-cultural is a *gift* and a *blessing*. The "mulattos" of this world, he said, are the ones best equipped to lead us beyond the narrow confines of our tribal provinciality and into a creative, dynamic future as a multi-cultural global community.

It is my observation that the people who have done the most to advance God's Project in the world are those who have stood squarely and boldly in that central place of tension between two cultural realities and built bridges across the great divide. There was Moses, who could only have accomplished what he did because of his total immersion in the realities of both Pharaoh's palace and the Hebrew slave quarters. The Apostle Paul, who was able to navigate with the greatest of ease between the worlds of Greek philosophers and Hebrew prophets. Martin Luther King,

---

People who have done the most to advance God's Project in the world are those who have stood squarely and boldly in that central place of tension between two cultural realities and built bridges across the great divide.

Jr., whose boyhood home in Atlanta, Georgia, was situated literally on the dividing line between black and white communities. And, of course, Jesus of Nazareth, who has modeled for us most clearly of all what it means to be about God's Kingdom purposes, "on earth . . . as it is in heaven."

7.
GOSPEL MEETS CULTURE:
A West African evangelist provides clues for how it's done

My first encounter with the Dida people of south-central Ivory Coast came on a weekend visit to the village of Yocoboué in July 1979. I had been invited there along with my wife, Jeanette, and colleagues, David and Wilma Shank, to begin discussions about what our mission agency might be willing to contribute to the vision of a Bible school for training church leaders in the Harrist Church throughout the Dida region.

The rather arduous, late rainy-season trip from the capital city of Abidjan to Yocoboué in the central forest region took us nearly four hours. It proved worthwhile, however, from the moment we approached the outskirts of the village and discovered the entire church choir waiting patiently "since early morning" to accompany us in song and dance to our place of meeting.

> Harris' ministry lasted a mere 18 months.
> During this brief period, however, an estimated
> 100,000 to 200,000 people accepted the
> evangelist's call, received baptism, and took
> their first steps toward a new life in Christ.

As we gathered late in the afternoon to review upcoming activities planned for the weekend, a passing comment from our host, Dominique, served as our first indicator that we were in for, among other things, a musical feast. "The processional songs you heard out there on the road earlier today," he informed us, "are what we call *nouveautés*. They are songs composed only recently by young people within the church. Tonight, however, when the sun goes down, we will gather at the preacher's house for a concert of *dogbro* music, our really old and powerful songs, dating back to the early years when the gospel was first preached in these parts by the Prophet Harris."

The "messenger of Christ" who started it all

In 1913, nearly seven decades before our visit to Yocoboué, William Wade Harris, a 53-year-old West African prophet-evangelist, left his native Liberia and stepped across the French colonial border into neighboring Ivory Coast. He was equipped with little more than a passionate desire to share the good news of Jesus. Walking barefoot from village to village for hundreds of miles along the coast, Harris challenged people everywhere to lay aside their traditional objects of worship and turn instead to the one, true God.

> *The sky and the earth were in such close proximity, in fact, that people actually had to walk around bent over, for if they were to stand fully upright, their heads would hit the sky.*

Harris' ministry lasted a mere 18 months before he was arrested by the French regime, beaten, and sent packing back to Liberia. During this brief period, however, an estimated 100,000 to 200,000 people from over a dozen different ethnic groups, including the Dida, accepted the evangelist's call, received baptism, and took their first steps toward a new life in Christ.

The people Harris met along the way had had very little if any exposure to the Christian faith prior to his arrival. French Catholic missionaries had been working tirelessly for almost 20 years to establish a credible and lasting presence in the area, but had met with limited success. And the only Protestant influence in the region was to be found in a handful of African English-speaking clerks from neighboring countries who had come to Ivory Coast, not as missionaries but as agents of British trading companies.

So what was it about Harris' methods and message that produced such an astounding response from the local population? Two stories from his remarkable ministry provide us with clues.

The day God got a black eye

Many ethnic groups in West Africa have some kind of oral legends that describe the way things were, back in a blissful era "before time." Not infrequently, other legends recount what went drastically wrong to create the current mess we find ourselves in.

The Dida say that in the very beginning of time, the earth and the sky were very close together. Now the word for "sky" in Dida is also the principal word used for "God." And so it was that God and humans lived in close relationship with each other, literally never far out of reach, one from the other.

The sky and the earth were in such close proximity, in fact, that people actually had to walk around bent over, for if they were to stand fully upright, their heads would hit the sky. So close was the sky to the earth that a woman, whose hands became soiled in food preparation, never needed to go looking for a towel to wipe them on. She could simply reach up and wipe her hands on the sky.

Then one day an energetic Dida cook was pounding grain with a long pestle in a large wooden mortar-bowl. With every thump, thump, thump of the pounding action the pestle went higher and higher into the air, until finally it reached so high that it hit God in the eye. God was not happy, the story goes and, in an act of rage, declared for all to hear, "If that's the way these humans are going to treat me, then I'm going off to a far distant place and they can just come looking for me."

From that time onward, the Dida tried everything to reconnect with God. They sacrificed animals for appeasement. They sent messages through their departed ancestors and other spirits. One woman even got the idea that if she could just go and talk to God, she would be able to settle this matter and put things back in their proper place.

And so the woman fetched a large mortar-bowl, turned it upside down, and planted it firmly in the middle of her courtyard. Then she climbed up on top of it with the hope of reaching the heavens. But, alas, she discovered, the heavens were now too far away.

> *When Papa Dogui, my old friend in Yocoboué, told me this story, he slapped his knee and began to laugh until tears flowed down his cheeks.*

Not to be discouraged, the woman went around to all the neighboring courtyards and asked to borrow those households' mortars. When she had collected all she could find, she stacked them up, one on top of the other, until she had a gigantic pile reaching high into the heavens. Carefully, the woman climbed to the top of the pile, only to discover to her great disappointment, that she was still one mortar short—just *one short!*—of achieving her goal.

What to do? She climbed back down, looked at the pile, and said to herself, "I only need one more mortar. If I just slip one of these out from the bottom of the pile and place it very quickly at the top, I will have exactly what I need!" And so she gave it a try and . . . the entire pile came crashing down.

When Papa Dogui, my old friend in Yocoboué, told me this story, he slapped his knee and began to laugh until tears flowed down his cheeks. Then, wiping his face, he leaned forward with renewed vigor and said, "That's what made the message of Harris so powerful! It was Harris who told us that our ancestors had gotten the story only partly right. Maybe it was out of ignorance. More likely out of shame. For whatever reasons, when our ancestors offended God, they ran and hid in the forest behind the trees. And God came looking for them to make things right. If there is no peace with God, Harris said, it is not *God's* fault; it's *our* fault. God has tried *everything* to get through to us, even sending his son Jesus to show us the way."

Then pausing for a moment, Papa Dogui looked at me and asked, "Is it any wonder that when we heard these words, we agreed to give up our objects of worship and receive baptism at the hands of Harris?"

"Teach us the songs of heaven!"

William Wade Harris was a man on the move, never staying long in any one location. In some instances, villagers would travel great distances to hear him preach, receive his baptism, then return home all in the same day, never to see him again.

How much these early believers really understood about Christian faith is hard to know. But for those who lingered long enough to capture more of his teaching, Harris did what he could to ensure a sound foundation by introducing them to the Ten Commandments, the Apostles' Creed, and the Lord's Prayer. Additional advice he offered included counsel on husband-wife relationships, intertribal conflict, Christ-like attitudes toward the oppressive French colonial government, ideas for worship, and suggestions on how to select the preachers and 12 apostles who would give spiritual leadership to the scores of newly emerging faith communities.

One of the questions frequently asked of Harris by new converts during those brief encounters concerned the type of music that they were expected to sing once they arrived back home in their villages. "Teach us the songs of heaven," they pleaded with him, "so that we can truly bring glory to God."

Now it is important to understand something of Harris' background in order to appreciate his response to the thousands of new believers who crowded around him, clinging almost desperately to every word of counsel he could give them. David A. Shank's book, *Prophet Harris, the "Black*

William Wade Harris, 1860-1929.

Elijah" of West Africa, describes in considerable detail the early years of Harris' life and only increases our amazement at the truly innovative approach Harris took to this matter.

Born of a Methodist mother around 1860, Harris had spent over 35 years—nearly all of his pre-prophetic adult life (1873-1910)—attending and actively serving the so-called "civilized" Methodist and Episcopal churches of eastern Liberia. Quite understandably, the Western hymn traditions that filled the liturgies of these churches had come to be the sacred music dearly loved and cherished by Harris as well. When asked in 1978 whether Harris had any favorite hymns, his grandchildren recalled without hesitation, "Lo, He Comes with Clouds Descending" (his favorite hymn, which he sang repeatedly), "Guide Me, O Thou Great Jehovah," "Jesus, Lover of My Soul," "How Firm a Foundation," and "What a Friend We Have in Jesus."

Yet faced with the crowds seeking his advice on this most important issue, Harris refused easy answers. "I have never been to heaven," he wisely told them, "so I cannot tell you what kind of music is sung in God's royal village. But know this," he continued, "that God has no personal favorite songs. He hears all that we say in whatever language. It is sufficient for us to compose hymns of praise to him with our own music and in our own language for him to understand."

When asked further how exactly they were to proceed in composing these new "songs of God," Harris told the people to begin by using the music and dance forms with which they were already acquainted. For the Dida people—one of the first and largest ethnic groups to feel the impact of Harris' ministry—this represented a remarkable repertoire of at least 30 distinct classifications of tradition-

> *"That's it!" exclaimed Harris. "That is the music you must work with! Though now you must refrain from using these songs for earthly rulers and lesser spirits and begin transforming the words bit by bit in order to bring glory to God."*

al musical genres, ranging from love ballads and funeral dirges to songs composed for hunting, rice planting, and rendering homage to wealthy community leaders.

Not all musical genres, however, were suitable, according to Harris, for use in praising God. In the Dida village of Lauzoua, not far from Yocoboué, a woman-musician stepped forward and began singing for Harris a *zlanje* tune, a kind of traditional love song with suggestive lyrics aimed at seducing potential partners into sexual activity. "That song does not honor God," Harris said. "Sing something else."

So another singer came forward proposing a *dogbro* tune, a type of "praise song" that literally hurls forth or shouts out the name of a nature spirit, a wealthy family head, or clan leader deserving special attention or recognition. "That's it!" exclaimed Harris. "That is the music you must work with! Though now you must refrain from using these songs for earthly rulers and lesser spirits and begin transforming the words bit by bit in order to bring glory to God."

Encouraged by this counsel from Harris, the new believers returned home to Yocoboué and other surrounding villages and set to work composing hymns of praise to God. One such early hymn proclaims:

It was the Lord who first gave birth to us and
    placed us here.
How were we to know
That the Lord would give birth to us a second time?
Thanks to Him, we can live in peace on this earth!

In the years that followed Harris' swift passage throughout southern Ivory Coast, Dida composers explored other
themes and developed additional musical styles as they
learned to read the Scriptures and grew in Christian understanding. Some of these hymns tell Bible stories or relate events from the history of what became the Harrist
movement. Other texts function as prayers, mini-sermons,
and confessions of faith—all set to music by members of
the Dida church, for the Dida church, and in a language
that the Dida church can well understand.

The opening lines of the Apostles' Creed, when adapted
by one Harrist hymn composer, take the following form:

My God, our Father, Almighty, Almighty,
Creator of the heavens and the earth,
It is He who is Truth, our Father alone.
And it is Jesus who is our Defender.
As for the Holy Spirit sent by Jesus,
He is Life and Healing for us all.

While our family lived among the Dida in the 1980s, it
was my rare privilege to work with Harrist leaders at col-
lecting and transcribing over 500 hymn texts from the oral
worship traditions of the church, spanning the 75-year period from 1913 to 1988. Since our departure from Ivory
Coast in 1996, scores of new compositions have been
added to the church's repertoire, and these, in several new
musical styles that did not even yet exist during our years
of worshiping with the Harrist community.

Four things will happen when gospel meets culture

William Wade Harris was a truly incredible gospel communicator, living as he did in that central point of tension between the "newspaper" of West African culture and the biblical story of God's Big Project to "reconcile all things to himself in Jesus Christ."

Though Harris may not have been able to articulate it in so many words, he also knew intuitively what all effective gospel communicators have always known—that several things are likely to happen within a given culture when that culture and God's Project meet.

I think of these things as the four "Cs" of the gospel/culture encounter. They are *continuation, correction, completion,* and *creation.*

Continuation. The first thing that happens when gospel meets culture is that . . . nothing happens! The Dida-speaking people living in south central Ivory Coast continue just as before to speak the Dida language and to live in south-central Ivory Coast.

They also continue to roll off their beds or sleeping mats at about 5:30 each morning, walk out into the moist pre-dawn air, greet the elders in the family courtyard, pick up their machetes and head out on foot to the fields for a

---

William Wade Harris lived in that central point of tension between the "newspaper" of West African culture and the biblical story of God's Big Project to "reconcile all things to himself in Jesus Christ."

day's work. They continue to labor hard until early afternoon when the sun becomes unbearable, and then head back to the village with babies on their backs and freshly-trapped bush meat and other harvested produce on their heads. They continue to look forward to that time each day in late afternoon when the setting sun provides relief from the blistering heat, when the sounds and smells of pounding pestles and boiling kettles fill the air, and when families gather to partake of generous portions of *foutou banane* and *sauce graine* before turning in for the night.

These are simply things that Dida people *are* and *do*, and there is no reason in the world why any of them should change when the Dida decide to embrace God's offer of *shalom* in their lives.

Correction. There are, however, a number of things that *are* likely to change. A new awareness of being created in God's image, for example, will almost certainly raise questions about the appropriateness of chopping a young female victim in two for the purposes of sealing a peace covenant between two warring villages. Or of hiding objects for protection under one's bed at night if Jesus is now "our Defender and Keeper." When the impact of God's Project is fully realized within a culture, some former beliefs just become unbelievable. Some actions, undoable. Some songs, unsingable. Laws are not usually required to forbid such activities. They simply no longer make sense, no longer fit with the new reality. And so they drop off, become irrelevant, disappear, or fade away.

Completion. Then there are those things that are neither carried over intact, nor outright discontinued and abandoned. They are things that are modified and ultimately transformed—sometimes rapidly, sometimes gradually—never to be the same again.

> *Within 10 years of the movement's origins,
> youthful composers in the church were
> "singing a new song," having created an
> entirely new musical style that seemed literally
> to burst forth from the hearts of this second
> generation of believers.*

The *dogbro* hymn texts would fit this category. Beginning with a solid base in Dida life and culture as praise songs addressed to particular spirits or village notables worthy of special attention, these songs take on a whole new meaning and, in some senses, "find their fulfillment" when they become focused on God. One of Yocoboué's first preachers counseled the early hymn composers with these words, "God is not just another chief for whom songs must be written. God is THE Chief of *all* the chiefs! So however the *dogbro* songs were used in former days to bring honor and glory to their subjects, they must now be that much better since it is God, the Lord of All, whom we are praising!"

Creation. And finally there are certain things never before existing that simply spring up out of nowhere as obvious and necessary in light of life's new realities. The Dida, for example, had never before heard of preachers prior to the coming of Harris into their lives. Yet this role became an essential one in the post-Harris period for the new faith communities who wanted to keep God's Project faithfully on track.

It is also interesting to note that the *dogbro* hymns, while playing an important transitional role in providing early worship forms for the church, eventually gave way to whole new musical initiatives that could no longer be contained in the "old wineskins." By the mid-1920s, within 10 years of the movement's origins, youthful composers in the church were "singing a new song," having created an entirely new musical style that seemed literally to burst forth from the hearts of this second generation of believers.

Bringing it on home

Missionaries have sometimes been labeled as culture-bashers, and in certain instances, the accusations have no doubt been justified. In reality, however, what happens when gospel encounters culture is a far more complex set of dynamics than is often recognized.

The easiest role for any of us to play in all of this is as armchair quality controllers, sitting outside someone else's culture and offering advice as to how change should or shouldn't happen. Changes *will* happen. Of that much we can be certain. But what should those changes be? In which order of priorities? On what timetable? And under whose watchful eye?

Before we become too convinced about what God wants to do in someone else's backyard, we need to take a closer look at the place where God has planted us. For us the key question is what should be happening when God's Project comes into *our* cultural context? What parts of that culture can be carried over? What is no longer compatible with God's *Shalom*-Making Plan and needs serious correction? What can be transformed to become of greater value in promoting God's cause in the world? And what has not even yet been created that is necessary for God's purposes to be fully realized?

Only then, when we have gained some perspective on ourselves by asking these hard questions about our own

> *Before we become too convinced about what
> God wants to do in someone else's backyard,
> we need to take a closer look at the place where
> God has planted us.*

cultural realities, do we have any integrity at all in participating in the much needed broader discussions of what it means to become God's global faith family . . . together.

8.
PEOPLE
ENCOUNTERS:
From coercing and cloning to "commending Jesus"

At first I couldn't believe my eyes. It had been a mighty long time since I had seen so many white faces, all crammed into one place.

It was May of 1986. I was returning home from the clinic in Abidjan, Ivory Coast, where Jeanette had just given birth to our third child, Mary Laura. On a whim, I decided to make a quick stop at the Hotel Ivoire bookshop to pick up a daily newspaper.

This was ordinarily a relatively painless exercise. Five minutes and you're on your way. But not today. As I entered the hotel lobby, my rapid walking pace slowed to a crawl as I made my way through a teeming throng of bubbly, boisterous tourists. All Americans, I discovered.

How many of them are there? I wondered. And what brings them to Abidjan? One eager couple—we'll call them

> *"And the fun part," chimed in Bill, "is that you have no idea where in the world you're going until they open the airplane door and you hop out on the runway. Ain't that great?"*

Bill and Thurma—right off the plane from Colorado Springs—were more than willing to supply me with some answers.

"There are 800 of us," they told me. "We're part of a tour group called Surprise Safaris."

"Surprise Safaris?" I asked. "What's that all about?"

"You've never heard of Surprise Safaris?" they exclaimed. "Wow! We've been traveling with them for almost 15 years now. Been to 45 countries in them 15 years. Never expected retirement would be so much fun!"

"So, how does all this work?" I wanted to know.

"Well, it's really pretty simple," said Thurma. "You pay Surprise Safaris $1,500 per trip, no matter where the organizers decide to take you."

"And the fun part," chimed in Bill, "is that you have no idea where in the world you're going until they open the airplane door and you hop out on the runway. Ain't that great? We've been to Brazil, Singapore, the Canary Islands . . . well, here, look at these!" Bill reached deep into his pants pocket and pulled out a string of 45 badges representing all of the countries they had managed to visit.

"So, what do you think of Ivory Coast?" I asked.

"Well, actually this trip was apparently supposed to go to Tunisia. You know, over there by Khadafy. But the word leaked out and everybody started canceling. So we ended up here. Ivory Coast? To be honest with you, I had never heard of Ivory Coast before. When we landed at the airport and I saw the sign, 'Welcome to Ivory Coast,' I said, where in the heck is *that*? The guy sitting next to us thought it must be somewhere in Africa, and guess what, it is!"

"So, do you plan to do some exploring while you're here?" I asked.

"Exploring? Oh, no, there won't be any time for that. They've got everything pretty much planned out for us. And they don't like us to go wandering off by ourselves. It's just not safe in a lot of these places, you know. There *is* one shopping day, I think, but for that they're bringing some of the local craftspeople with their stuff right here into the hotel lobby so we don't need to go downtown to the market and take a chance of getting mugged or something."

As we were speaking, Thurma moved over to the postcard rack and with great gusto began plucking off one of every card on display. "She always goes for the complete collection," Bill explained. "Sometimes we end up with two or three hundred postcards per trip. In Hong Kong we had to buy an extra carry-on bag just to get all the cards back home."

I was about to bid farewell to Bill and Thurma when a very attractive young Ivorian woman passed by. "Wow!" exclaimed Bill, just loud enough for Thurma to hear. "She's one of the prettiest gals I've ever seen . . . next to my wife . . . 'course some of those gals I didn't see next to my wife!"

Thurma's eyes hit the ceiling. Not so much with embarrassment. More like boredom. She had clearly heard that line from Bill before. Back in Colorado. And probably in Brazil. In Singapore. The Canary Islands. And in most of the other ports-of-call that Surprise Safaris had provided.

I went to the back of the store, picked up a newspaper, and returned to Bill and Thurma. "Well, I guess I need to be going," I said. "Have a great time in Ivory Coast."

> *Crazy, I thought, how God has granted to certain people—and to Americans, in particular, it seems—the remarkable capacity of "learning to know someone" without actually knowing one single significant thing about them.*

"Hey, yeah, we sure will," they said. "It's been great learning to know you!"

As I made my way back through the crowd and outside to my waiting car, I wondered what Bill and Thurma had meant by their last statement to me—"It's been great learning to know you." Neither of them had shown the slightest interest during our brief encounter in finding out who I was or what this fellow compatriot of theirs might be doing in Ivory Coast. Crazy, I thought, how God has granted to certain people—and to Americans, in particular, it seems—the remarkable capacity of "learning to know someone" without actually knowing *one* single significant thing about them.

If you're looking to live in cultural isolation, better move to another planet

I suppose there are still some folks out there somewhere who imagine a world in which they can live in total isolation from people culturally different from themselves. To these dear folk I simply say: Good luck. That world is rapidly shrinking with each passing day.

In my relatively small midwestern hometown of Elkhart, Indiana (population 52,000), there are now over 40 languages spoken by students in the public school system.

Languages with the largest number of speakers are Spanish, Lao, Khmer, Arabic, Gujarati and Urdu (both from India), Mandarin, and Korean. Other smaller groupings include a smattering of European languages (Greek, Portuguese, Italian, German, etc.), as well as Sotho (South Africa), Chicewa (Malawi), Tagalog (Philippines), Amoy (China), Kinyarwanda (Rwanda), Amharic (Ethiopia), and Ibo (Nigeria).

Elkhart is, of course, a microcosm of America as a whole. A few quick statistics can help paint the picture of the future toward which we are moving.

• More than 120 million Americans, not including African Americans, identify themselves as belonging to one of 500 ethnic groups present in the country. In addition to learning or already speaking English, these members of our society communicate in one or more of 636 languages and dialects.

• The high school graduating class of 2004 is the most racially and ethnically diverse of any class in U.S. history. Twenty percent of the graduates had at least one first-generation immigrant parent. And 10 percent had a parent who was a non-citizen.

• California's population is no longer of predominantly white European origin. Asians, African Americans, and Hispanics now comprise more than half of the state's population. This will also be true for Arizona by 2005, for Texas by 2010, and for the nation as a whole by the year 2050.

The issue is not *whether* there will be cross-cultural encounters in our future, but *what kind*.

Cross-cultural encounters come in all shapes and sizes

Individuals who come in contact with people of other cultures, whether on North American soil or in international contexts elsewhere around the world, often react in one of two ways to such encounters. Put in simplest terms, there are those who conclude that "we and they are different," and others who determine that "we and they are the same." Both perspectives contain some elements of truth. Yet both are insufficient as explanations for what happens when two peoples meet.

"We and they are different." The most obvious first reaction when one climbs off the plane in some strange place is to note how different everything is from life back home. Things just don't *look* the same, *sound* the same, or *smell* the same. My wife and I learned this several years ago when we accompanied a church youth group from Elkhart to a national youth convention in Oregon. Within 24 hours of our arrival, the youth in our company had determined "they just don't make Mountain Dew in Oregon the same way they do back in Indiana."

Now it is one thing to simply observe that differences exist; it is quite another to apply value judgments to those differences. Here are a few examples of how relationships and reality in general can become distorted when that next step is taken:

- **Paternalism—"We are superior to them."** Arrogance and disdain sometimes result when different peoples meet. Taking a noonday siesta in a given culture might be interpreted by the visiting outsider as laziness; holding one's fork in the left hand as impractical; conducting worship services that continue non-stop for five hours as excessive and out of control; and driving on the left side

> *The issue is not* whether *there will be cross-cultural encounters in our future, but* what kind.

of the road as unsafe or downright stupid. Most people who bring this kind of attitude with them when encountering other cultures are impatient to get back home where life can return to normal once again.

- **Romanticism—"They are superior to us."** Some starry-eyed travelers come away from cross-cultural encounters totally enchanted by the people and perspectives they have met. Quite opposite from those who look upon others with disgust, these people are mesmerized by cultures other than their own and have difficulty seeing anything in them but the good, the right, and the noble. Whatever words of complaint or criticism one hears from these people are usually directed at their own native culture for which they have little patience, tolerance, or hope.

- **Separatism—"We are fine without them."** "Okay," others say, "so we're different. That's the way it should be. We don't particularly like *their* way of doing things. And they probably don't like *ours*. That's fine. No one here is right or wrong, better or worse. We're just . . . different. God made diversity and pronounced it good. Let's keep it that way."

"We and they are the same." At the other end of the spectrum are those who prefer to emphasize what they have in common with people they meet. And there certainly are commonalities. Eugene A. Nida and others have

Third-world seen through first-world eyes.

helpfully pointed out that certain basic drives, for example, can be found across the entire human family—the drives of thirst, hunger, and sex; of loving and being loved;
of physical, mental, and aesthetic activity. More, in fact,
unites us as human beings than divides us. That is a simple fact. But *simple* turns *simplistic* when the deep cultural differences existing between "us" and "them" are re-
garded as insignificant, irrelevant, or even virtually
nonexistent, for all practical purposes. When this happens, distortions of the following nature are likely to appear:

- **Provincialism—"They are basically like us."** People
  who choose, for whatever reason, not to take culture seriously spend little time trying to analyze either their
  own culture or anyone else's. So they have little option
  but to assume that people everywhere view the world
  much the same way they do. When an elderly gentleman in the village of Yocoboué asks me whether, in my
  view, it is better for a husband to demand a chicken or

a bottle of gin as payment from his wife, should he catch her having an adulterous affair, he is assuming that husbands where I come from require payments in such instances. He also takes for granted that chickens and gin are items of high value in my culture, bringing them to the top of my preferred list. Likewise, when singer Mariah Carey says, "Whenever I watch TV and see those poor starving kids all over the world, I can't help but cry. I mean I'd love to be skinny like that, but not with all those flies and death and stuff," she is making an assumption that one thing all people everywhere *must* share in common is their desire to be skinny. She implies that the "flies and death and stuff" are just marginal detractors from an otherwise not-so-dismal situation.

- **Reductionism—"Us and them, we are the world."**
Another way to downplay the significance of cultural differences is to assume that we could all get along and make a better world for ourselves as a happy human family if we would just do or be the right thing together. Advertisements confirm this for us on a daily basis. "If I could teach the world to sing in perfect harmony" . . . while drinking Coca Cola . . . that'd be "the *real* thing." (The smiling faces of satisfied Coke-guzzling Tibetan monks and Kenyan cattle herders are the ultimate proof that it *must* be true.) Offering another solution is cable TV mogul Ted Turner who went on record several years ago announcing his belief that commonly shared news stories and televised images might well be our best hope for bringing the world together. Others aren't so sure CNN will ever pull this off. For them, it's Microsoft. Rock music. Olympic sports. The English language. Or the American way of life.

So what's this got to do with God's Big Project to make peace with the world?

There is nothing more devastating to God's *Shalom-Making* Project than when those called to be The Project's primary model and messengers succumb to the attitudes and approaches described in the preceding pages. The sad truth is, however, that much of church history could be written to chronicle precisely that.

When God's people throughout history have adopted paternalistic, romanticized, separatist, provincial, or reductionist attitudes towards people of other faiths or cultures, four corresponding actions have usually followed as natural outgrowths of those attitudes:

Crush. One way to deal with people different from oneself is simply to exterminate them. Saul of Tarsus, as a zealous first-century Jewish missionary, was quite convinced that "the only *good* Christians were *dead* ones." He was in the process of tracking them down when he met Jesus on the road to Damascus (Acts 9). It is interesting that Saul, who later became Paul, never again raised a sword against people failing to accept his point of view. His encounter with the Crucified Lord simply wouldn't permit it. That key insight was apparently lost, however, on the 8th century "Christian" ruler Charlemagne when he ordered that "any Saxon who refuses to accept baptism should be put to death." Or the 16th-century cross-bearing conquistador who declared, "Who can deny that the use of gunpowder against pagans is the burning of incense to our Lord?" Or the 17th-century New England Puritans who wiped out hundreds of recalcitrant native Pequot tribespeople—and this, during the very period when they were organizing a "holy" colony based on biblical principles and values.

> *The human impulse is enormous to elevate one's own cultural patterns and see them reproduced in others.*

Coerce. The most extreme form of coercion is Charlemagne's, "Be baptized or die!" But aside from this, there are other, sometimes more subtle, forms that can and have been used to draw converts into the faith—manipulation, deceit, trickery, inducement, misrepresentation, intimidation, bribery, enforcement, enslavement, incarceration, torture, and even banishment from the human community. If ever and whenever these tactics are employed by Christians in their life and witness to the world, "good news" turns quickly into "bad news." And God's message of *shalom* is distorted beyond recognition and betrayed to its very core.

Clone. The human impulse is enormous to elevate one's own cultural patterns and see them reproduced in others. Not surprisingly, "Christianizing" and "Civilizing" have often gone hand in hand. Sometimes this has happened in a very deliberate and intentional manner. Such was the case, says Lakota/Sioux writer and speaker, Richard Twiss, when mission boarding schools were created in the United States at the turn of the 20th century. Native American children were relocated from their homes and placed in surroundings where the old "savage" ways could fade away and gradually be replaced by the practices and principles of White civilization. God had made a mistake when He made them Indians, the children were told, and now that mistake was going to be corrected. It would be necessary to "kill the Indian," as one official put it, in order to "save the man."

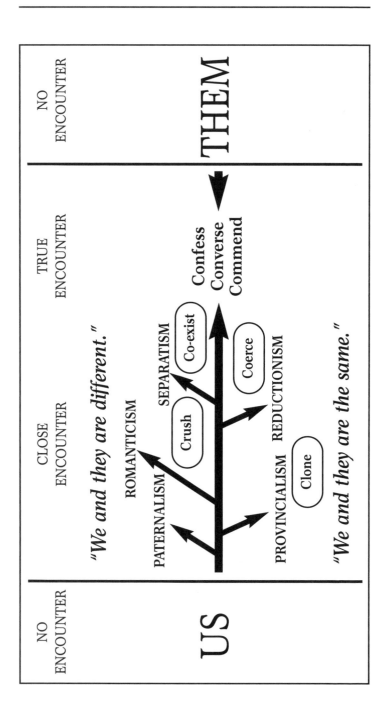

Co-exist. There are many reasons why people of different cultures choose to live in communities separate from one another. Sometimes there are language barriers. Sometimes there is fear. Sometimes there are legalized and institutionalized forms of racism. It is not particularly encouraging to learn that despite the growing diversity of peoples and cultures in America today, we are making virtually no progress in creating a truly integrated society. Most research indicates, in fact, that the various cultural communities making up American society today live more segregated from each other than they did a decade ago.

It would be wonderful to at least be able to report some level of progress on America's alleged "most segregated hour in the week"—the time roughly between 10:00-11:00 a.m. on Sunday morning when large numbers of Americans are at worship. Unfortunately, here too, it would appear, we continue to live more as foreigners and strangers to each other, than as "fellow-citizens," "joint heirs," and "equal members" of the family of God, "being built *together* with all the others into a place where God lives through his Spirit" (Ephesians 2:11-19).

Getting from here to there will require a few C-changes

We have a lot of hard work to do if we are to move from our current "non-encounters" or *close* encounters to the *real* encounters that will be necessary for us to participate fully in God's Big Reconciling Project. We can start to move in the right direction by taking a few simple steps.

Confess. Most everybody in the world seems to know what some Christians refuse to admit: The church is not a perfect body. It makes mistakes, sometimes very big ones. It has not always managed, despite hard work and good in-

> *Far too often, the* methods *used in transmitting the gospel have contradicted the* message *of God's peacemaking initiative in Jesus.*

tentions, to live up to its calling as model and messenger of God's plan to set things right with the world. In the worst of cases, it is in fact *because* of God's people—to adapt slightly one of the apostle Paul's stinging observations— that unbelievers actually speak evil of God (Romans 2:24). Now *that* hurts! But if it is true, then the church has some serious repenting and rectifying to do. Nothing less can gain the credibility she needs to represent God's truly remarkable plan with integrity. For that plan involves breaking down walls and building bridges between peoples who harbor feelings of deep-seated hostility toward each other and toward God.

Converse. Once Christians begin to recognize their own ongoing, desperate need for God's grace and forgiveness in their lives, they suddenly discover they have some good news worthy of a conversation. A *conversation*—not a monologue, not a sermon or a speech, but as the dictionary defines it "a pleasant, often friendly act or instance of talking together, of exchanging ideas and opinions." Conversations, we know, require at least two partners in dialogue, partners who bring their own life experiences to the table, expecting to learn and contribute mutually in the process. You can win a war. You can win a debate. But you can never win—or lose, for that matter—a conversation. People who turn nasty when conversing with others, who demean, manipulate, disrespect, or in some way humiliate their partners in dialogue, have only one thing to lose: the conversation partners themselves. And when this happens, there is often little hope of ever gaining them back again.

Commend. The landscape of history is cluttered with ill-fated attempts to impose the Christian faith on unsuspecting, unwilling recipients and to clone them into something other than what they were created to be. Far too often, the *methods* used in transmitting the gospel have contradicted the *message* of God's peacemaking initiative in Jesus. In such instances, the church has communicated a message falsely perverse and counter-intuitive to what God is actually up to in the world.

The decision to embrace or reject God's love in Jesus is and must always remain fundamentally a *voluntary* one. And so, in the words of Kenneth Cragg, Anglican bishop and professor of Islamic studies, the church continues to do the only thing she *can* do—she "commends Jesus." Nothing more, nothing less. Not by might, nor by force. But in the spirit of the Prince of Peace by whom she lives and for whom she is prepared to die.

9.
GLOBAL
FAITH FAMILY:
Christianity, really?
You mean
someone still cares?

I sometimes think that the greatest miracle of all time is the survival of the gospel message, despite all the nasty things that have been done in its name. How amazing, in many respects, to find the gospel not simply surviving in our world today, but in fact *thriving*—alive and well! Can there be any better proof of God's sense of humor? Of God's unflappable determination to see the reconciling message of Jesus get through, sometimes *because of*, but also *in spite of*, the human instruments to whom the communication of that message has been entrusted?

From the West to the rest . . . and back again

It was a beautiful spring day in Paris in late May 2004. I had come to the French *métropole* with a number of my co-workers to participate in a consultation focusing on the state of the church in Europe.

It was Sunday morning, the last day of the consultation. We had been invited to worship at the Evangelical Assembly of the Rock, one of more than a hundred African "immigrant churches" found today in the cultural and political capital of the once far-flung French colonial empire.

How ironic, I thought, in this predominantly Catholic country which for so many years sent forth missionaries to distant outposts around the world, that now less than 20 percent of children born here are actually presented for baptism—down from 75 percent in 1970. Additionally, regular church attendance among adults is in free-fall decline in France today, currently estimated at only seven percent of the population.

All the more amazing, then, for our visiting group, as we wound our way from the bus stop in Montreuil-Sous-Bois, an eastern suburb of Paris, through the streets of this lower-income section of the city, to hear the music. The richly blended choral harmonies and the pulsating beat of drums penetrated through the outer walls of the converted factory warehouse which served as a meeting place for the congregation that was hosting us for the day.

Yet, the greatest surprise awaited us inside. For here we were to discover a vibrant community of faith, 300-strong, gathering from across the city for a day of fellowship and worship. Unlike the graying membership of most Euro-

Unlike the graying membership of most European Christian communities today, this place was filled with youth and children.

pean Christian communities today, this place was filled with youth and children, "a congregation with an average age in the mid-thirties," according to Pastor Miangu Mas Félicien, who greeted us warmly upon our arrival.

Brightly colored banners decorated the walls of the spacious worship hall, proclaiming the faith of the assembled believers: "Jesus is Lord!" "Jesus, King of Kings!" "Hello, Holy Spirit!" And spilling down over the pulpit, emblazoned boldly on a strip of African cloth, was a six-letter word— S-H-A-L-O-M—placed there, it seemed, as a reminder for worshipers of what was at the core of the gospel message.

Positioned front and center, in a place high above the platform where intergenerational women's choirs were holding forth, was yet another statement of faith: "Jesus Reigns Over All The Nations!" Certainly *no* declaration could have appeared more true on this day as worshippers streamed into the building, representing 17 countries from across the African continent and around the world. They came from Angola, Benin, Cameroon, Central African Republic, Congo-Brazzaville, Democratic Republic of Congo, Gabon, Ivory Coast, Tunisia, Nigeria, Uganda, Senegal, Togo, from the French overseas departments of Guadeloupe, Martinique, and French Guiana, and from France itself.

"Our goal is to build a truly multicultural church," Pastor Mas told us. "Living here in France as immigrants in exile, far from the social, tribal, and national conflicts we so often experience in Africa, offers us the unique opportunity to break down the walls of class and ethnic division and truly become the church God wants us to be."

But that's not all. The vision Pastor Mas has for his burgeoning congregation is much larger than simply trying to create a spiritual home for Africans living on foreign soil. "We are called as God's people," he told us, "to move be-

> *If expansion of the church continues at the present rate, Africa may well be on the pathway to surpass all other continents as the largest heartland of the Christian faith.*

yond the walls of our worship hall and to be the 'salt of the earth' to our European brothers and sisters, spiritually paralyzed by secularism and relativism. We want to challenge them to rediscover the true values of the gospel."

The pastor paused. "Do you remember the counsel of the Old Testament prophet Isaiah: 'Cast your bread upon the waters and it will come back to you'?" he asked. "Well, we are the fulfillment of that prophetic word, the bread cast long ago that is now returning. The church you see today is the harvest of seeds planted many generations ago. And now, that harvest is in turn producing a whole new batch of seeds ready to be used by God for replanting right here in Europe."

The amazing rise of the Southern church

The vision and vigor manifested by Pastor Mas and the vibrant Evangelical Assembly of the Rock on the outskirts of Paris is but a small window into a much larger trend that has been taking place on a worldwide scale in recent years, quietly but forcefully under our unsuspecting noses.

The case of Africa is an interesting one to note. In 1900, the number of Christians on the continent was estimated at roughly 10 million, or about nine percent of the continent's total population. In 1950, that number had grown to 34 million, or about 15 percent of the total. In 1965, we were looking at 75 million Christians, or one-quarter of the

> *Despite the colossal significance of the Church's southward shift, little or none of this has proven to be of much importance to people living in the traditional heartlands of Christianity.*

African populace. And by 2000, that figure had exploded to 360 million, or nearly half of the continent's inhabitants.

Today, Africa holds, without rival, "the distinction of being the place where the largest number of people have moved into the Christian stream of history in the shortest amount of time," according to missiologist David A. Shank. Further, if expansion of the church continues at the present rate, Africa may well be on the pathway to surpass all other continents as the largest heartland of the Christian faith.

From a very different part of the world comes a report from David Aikman, a *Time* magazine international news correspondent for over two decades, who released his best seller, *Jesus in Beijing,* in 2003. In it, Aikman provides some rather shocking data about "how Christianity is transforming China and changing the global balance of power." If Christianity continues to grow at its current staggering rate, claims the reporter, one-third of China's population could be Christian within the next 30 years, making China one of the largest Christian nations in the world.

The remarkable story of what is happening in China and sub-Saharan Africa has its counterparts in other regions of the southern hemisphere. Based on the January 2005 statistics provided by David B. Barrett and Todd M. Johnson in their global census project which they update annually and publish in the *International Bulletin of Missionary Research,* roughly one-third of the world's population is today classified as part of the Christian family. Regional breakdowns of global church affiliation yield the following results, rounded off to the nearest million:

Latin America	623 million
Africa	596 million
Europe (including Russia)	514 million
Asia	498 million
North America	270 million
Oceania	27 million

If these figures can be accepted as trustworthy, then Christians living in the global South currently make up over two-thirds of the worldwide Christian family. And all indicators point to a future where that percentage will only increase, most likely in rather dramatic, substantial ways.

If God has such a great sense of humor, why aren't we laughing?

Several years ago I attended an evening concert given by a Congolese church choir on tour in the United States. About 45 minutes into the presentation, it was announced that the choir would be teaching the mostly white and slightly stiff middle-class audience a "sing-along song."

With a twinkle in his eye, the director turned to the crowd and said, "Now I know that for many of you, the music you've been hearing tonight likely has some strange harmonic patterns and a bit more rhythm and movement than you are used to. But let me tell you a secret. When we get to heaven, all of God's children are going to gather together and take a vote on what kind of music we're going to sing. Now you've probably heard about the incredible growth of the church in the global South. Well, guess who's going to win the vote? [The audience breaks out in hearty laughter.] So, if there's a chance you might be singing this kind of music *forever*, don't you think it would be a great idea to get started learning some of it right here *tonight?*"

The director's question was taken as it should have been, as a good-natured prodding and not a threat. But it had people talking after the performance, nonetheless. For some folks this was brand new information, fresh data just in from a galaxy somewhere beyond the Milky Way. For others it was a startling wake-up call, requiring some reshuffling of formerly held perceptions. For everyone else it was a healthy reminder of both the rapidly changing world in which we live, and the clear, new direction in which God's *Shalom*-Making Project is decidedly headed.

God, I believe, has an even greater sense of humor than this Congolese choir director, choosing to raise up from the world's so-called "dark continents" and "pagan lands" a dynamic new generation of people who have embraced The Cosmic Project and are on a sure course to carry it into the future.

What continues to amaze me, however, is that despite the colossal significance of the Church's southward shift happening right before our eyes, little or none of this has proven to be of much importance to people living in the traditional heartlands of Christianity. For most such folk, the prevailing stereotype of the "average Christian" in today's world remains the rather sorry, mid-20th century *Poisonwood Bible* missionary-type figure—white, male, old and cranky, privileged, paternalistic, and, by all clear indication, an archaic, tired breed of humanity.

Even in academic circles, where one would ordinarily expect a higher level of awareness and objectivity, the frequent lack of attentiveness to this matter, or unwillingness to acknowledge it, is often nothing short of astounding. At

Africa is on the pathway to becoming the largest heartland of the Christian faith.

the 1998 annual gathering of the African Studies Association meeting, for example, nearly 900 scholars converged on Chicago from around the world to give and receive nearly 900 presentations on the theme, "Africa's Encounter with the 20th Century." The papers were placed in 20 thematic sections: "Cultures and Cultural Change," "Gender and Sexuality," "Human Rights and Current Conflicts," and so on. Section D was devoted to the topic of "African Religions." Here, a total of 34 presentations were made. Of these, 23 dealt with Islam-related topics, seven with witchcraft, and four with issues loosely connected to the African church, grouped under the title, "Conflicted Conversions: Manifestations of Syncretism Among African Christians."

Hmmm. Four papers out of 900! And this despite the claim of contemporary church historian Adrian Hastings that, "Black Africa today is totally inconceivable apart from the presence of Christianity." Yet it apparently *was* for members of the ASA in 1998. And it was again two years later when the Association gathered in Nashville in 2000 for another annual meeting to grapple this time with the theme, "People and Power in 21st Century Africa." On this occasion, 11 out of 750 presentations touched on church-related issues—not exactly a powerhouse of research, but a decided improvement over the 1998 encounter. At least it showed a glimmer of hope for the future of the most important body of scholars in the entire Western hemisphere committed to monitoring current trends on the African continent!

"If I hadn't believed it, I would never have seen it with my own eyes."

We Euro-centric Westerners are in desperate need of the broader view, the bigger picture of what God is up to in the world. Sadly, at the very moment when a new spiritual family is being born, bringing together peoples from around the

> *We Euro-centric Westerners are in desperate*
> *need of the broader view, the bigger picture of*
> *what God is up to in the world.*

globe, we find ourselves retreating into a modern-day form of tribalism. We focus ever more narrowly on local agenda, constructing small-minded, culture-bound worldviews, nurturing individualized spiritualities, and growing increasingly out of touch with the religious trends shaping our planet. If we continue down this path, the outlook for our future is likely not too bright. In the course of time, we will almost certainly become marginalized by the stream of history and progressively irrelevant on the global scene, prattling on and on about self-important issues that matter less and less to more and more of the world's population.

It is a bitter pill for most Westerners to discover that we are no longer—if indeed we ever were—at the center of God's universe. Most of us, defying the usual order of scientific logic, will never *see* the true and profound significance of this new reality . . . until we *believe* it.

What will it be like to live in a world so different from anything we've ever seen or imagined:

- **a world** where the face of an "average global Christian" is that of a rural peasant woman working the rice fields of China, or an urban youth playing drums in a worship band in Santiago, Chile;

- **a world** where the majority of Christians are poor and, in many instances, experiencing some sort of hardship, opposition, or persecution for their faith;

- **a world** where nations with some of the largest Christian populations have names like Mexico, Nigeria, Philippines, and the Congo;

- **a world** where the centers of influence and gravity for the Church are shifting from London, Paris, and Rome to places like Lagos, Seoul, and Rio de Janeiro;

- **a world** where European nations like England, France, and Holland, highly unchurched and largely secularized, are declared urgent mission fields and find themselves receiving thousands of "foreign missionaries" from churches in dozens of countries, mostly in the global South.

We shouldn't tire ourselves out too much by trying to imagine what it would be like to live in such a world. This *is* our world! Right here. Right now.

God's Cosmic Peace-Making Project, seen from this global perspective, is not about to shrivel up, die out, or go away. Quite to the contrary, it has never been embraced by more people, never attracted followers from as many diverse cultural backgrounds, never been so full of youth and vigor. Never has there been a better opportunity to actually experience what the New Testament writer-evangelist, John, could have only imagined in the far-distant future when he saw "a large crowd of people, more than could be counted, coming from every race, tribe, nation, and language, and standing before the throne and before the Lamb" (Revelation 7:9).

> *We shouldn't tire ourselves out too much trying to imagine what it would be like to live in such a world. This is our world! Right here. Right now.*

What, then, shall we do with this surprising turn of events?

When one comes to a crossroads on a strange back-country road, it is generally best to slow down, look, and listen. We in the West, I believe, are at just such a cross-roads in regards to God's *shalom*-making initiative and the rapid pace with which it is finding a home in the hearts and lives of people around the world.

What are we to do with this new information? Let me suggest three principal options we have before us:

We can choose to *ignore* it. We're good at this. Whenever it suits our fancy. Or whenever news from outside our bounded set of preconceived ideas becomes too threatening for us to manage. Americans in particular need very little global information to get along quite nicely in the world, thank you very much. The Washington-based Pew Research Centre has produced surveys, for example, indicating that only 30 percent of Americans in the late 1990s expressed interest in news about other countries. And how did the events of September 11 affect those percentages? A follow-up survey done in September 2002 reported that the numbers actually *dropped*, that only 26 percent of Americans one year later followed foreign news "very closely," while 45 percent said international events had no effect on them. Trust me, if the tragic events of September 11 didn't pique our interest in world affairs, a couple hundred million conversions to Christianity in far-off China probably won't do it either.

We can choose to *deplore* it. It is not at all clear that most Westerners—and perhaps not even most Western *Christians*—will receive news about the growth of the Christian movement around the world with unbridled joy. I once heard Philip Jenkins, author of the remarkable book on

> *It is not at all clear that most Westerners will receive news about the growth of the Christian movement around the world with unbridled joy.*

global church trends, *The Next Christendom,* describe an encounter he had had with a frantic elderly woman at a church-related gathering. At the end of his presentation on the changing face of Christianity, the woman approached Jenkins in an almost desperate tone of voice and said, "You have told us about the rapid growth of the church in the Southern hemisphere, about the charismatic-style worship, the high regard for the Scriptures, the mission zeal, the belief in prophecy, healing, dreams, and visions, but, Mr. Jenkins, you haven't given us any ideas or suggestions on what we can do to *stop* it!"

We can choose to *explore* it. Okay, so this whole thing wasn't really supposed to happen. Following the demise of the Western colonial empires in the 1960s and 1970s, Christianity should have quietly returned back home or just disappeared along with the arrogant imperialists who imposed it on their unsuspecting subjects in the first place.

But it didn't. Instead, it was precisely at this point in the struggle for freedom, and the fresh energy generated around the building of new independent nation-states, that the gospel had its greatest appeal and began spreading almost wildly across the global South.

Now that alone should inspire us to look more closely at this thing we call "the gospel." And at the faithful, though imperfect, messengers who made that gospel known. And—perhaps most importantly—at the intriguing question of why Jesus and his gospel have so astoundingly prevailed where Christian-coated colonizers so dismally failed.

10.
VISION:
Still crazy after all these years

It has not been possible in these few pages to explore all of the hard questions about mission that confront us in our world today. This is just the beginning, not the end, of a long, but necessary conversation.

Many of the key questions we encounter are touched upon earlier in this book. As we draw our reflections to a close, let us review them briefly.

Questions about mission and why we need to face them

1. The problem. I believe that much uneasiness about mission today is rooted in three primary realties: our embarrassing mission *history*, our Western science-shaped *worldview*, and our *encounters* with people of other faiths—people who for many of us these days are simply the folks next door. How right *are* we, we find ourselves wondering. Is there *really* only one way to God? How can we be sure we aren't simply imposing our personal views on others?

> *We will need to come to terms with* this *simple question: Is there, in fact, a gospel to be communicated?*

What amazes me is how little these matters are openly discussed among Christian people and how seldom they are addressed in the teaching and preaching ministries of the church. Admittedly, the whole conversation is a bit of a threatening one. Hanging out one's dirty laundry, delving deeply into faith questions about one's beliefs and behaviors, and waking up to the realization that one's own native culture is today a mission field—these are not perspectives and activities most self-respecting people are likely to greet with great glee.

But do it we must. With honesty. And integrity. And a heightened sense of urgency. Our children are demanding it. Authentic participation in God's mission is requiring it. Anything less than serious attention devoted to these matters will result in a church ill-prepared for a multi-cultural world where inter-faith conversations are the norm and well-grounded gospel communicators, the great need.

2. The cosmic plan. But before we go any further, we will need to come to terms with *this* simple question: Is there, in fact, a gospel to be communicated? Many people in our culture—including increasing numbers of people in the church, it would seem—either don't think so or are having second thoughts about it.

At stake here is whether or not God is up to anything in the world that actually applies to *all* people, in every time and place. We have asserted in these pages that such is, in fact, the case:

- that God has a plan—a *cosmic* plan, to reconcile all things in the universe through Jesus Christ (Colossians 1:20);

- that this plan is *personal*, offered to each and every human being. That *all* people everywhere are invited to embrace and respond to God's peace-making initiative by receiving in their lives the gift of forgiveness, inner healing, and wholeness (Romans 5:1-2);

- that this plan is *social*, not just about isolated individuals, but about people estranged, in conflict or at war—people divided from other people by walls of hatred that in Jesus come tumbling down, opening a way to build bridges of understanding between former enemies and create communities of joy, grace, and peace (Ephesians 2:11-18).

Let's keep it simple. Either God's *Shalom*-Making Project in Jesus is for *all* people. Or it's not.

If it's not, than we are free to adopt the claims of other world religions or more localized sects. Or we may choose to piece together from a vast smorgasbord of spiritual resources our own custom-made religious experience of value only to me, as "my personal faith journey," or to that of my *family*, my *tribe* or my *nation*.

If, on the other hand, God's plan is designed and intended for the entire human race, then it is probably a wise thing to find out all we can about it—and about this "Jesus," through whom the plan is apparently being carried out.

3. Jesus. Several years ago I was asked to speak to a group of young adults who were exploring some of the "hard sayings" of Jesus. The saying to which I was assigned was the one found in John 14:6 where Jesus declares himself to be "the way, the truth, and the life." At one point in the conversation, one frustrated young man blurted out, "Wouldn't it be great if we just didn't have this verse in the Bible?

> *Let's keep it simple. Either God's* Shalom-Making *Project in Jesus is for* all *people. Or it's not.*

That would solve a lot of our problems on this matter, wouldn't it?"

Well, no, actually, it wouldn't. In fact, it likely wouldn't change much of anything at all. The decisive nature of the Jesus event in human history is not a one-isolated-verse affair. It is and always has been the central affirmation at the very heart of the gospel message right up until the present. "Regardless of what anyone may personally think or believe about him," writes Jaroslav Pelikan in *Jesus through the Centuries*, "Jesus of Nazareth has been the dominant figure in the history of Western culture for almost twenty centuries. If it were possible, with some sort of super-magnet, to pull up out of that history every scrap of metal bearing at least a trace of his name, how much would be left?"

Despite that, there have always been those who questioned the claims Jesus made about himself. Serious doubt and disbelief started already in Jesus' own lifetime when skeptics peppered him with penetrating questions: "Are you *really* the Messiah, the Son of God?" "Where does your authority come from?" "Who gave you the right to heal on the Sabbath?"

Now, as in the time of Jesus' earthly life and ministry, the single most important issue we have to face is: What will we do with Jesus? Everything else hinges on the response we are able to give to this central question.

4. Teaching, preaching, and healing. If we conclude that Jesus really is what he said, said what he meant, and meant what he said, then we'll have enough agenda to last us a lifetime. Suddenly, everything about Jesus becomes

important to us. No, not just important. Life-altering. Priority-shaping. All-determining.

If Jesus truly is the message and means by which God has chosen to set things right with our troubled world, then we'll be watching him with utmost attentiveness to see what this *"shalom-*in-the-flesh" looks like. And as we keep our eyes and ears focused on Jesus:

- The *Truth* he speaks will begin to transform our minds.

- The *Way* he walks will put our feet into action.

- The *Life* he offers will fill our hearts with gratitude and praise.

This is the life of a disciple, patterning one's whole life and energies after those of the Master's. Whatever was good enough for Jesus as God's primary *Shalom*-Maker in the world will be more than good enough for us. If Jesus "brought good news to the poor," this becomes our assignment. If he "proclaimed liberty to the captives," we commit ourselves to the task. If he sends us forth to "make disciples of all nations," we pack our bags and prepare for departure.

Evangelism, service, peace-making, justice-building— these are *not* words, to rephrase Paul McCartney, that "go together well" for most followers of Jesus. But they should. And they must. If we want to follow in Jesus' footsteps. And participate in God's mission the way Jesus demonstrated it should be done.

5. The church. The church, unfortunately, has not always made God's work in the world a reputable, smooth-running operation. Okay, *that's* an understatement. The church has sometimes botched and bungled the whole thing . . . bodaciously.

Admittedly, the entire project got off to a rather shaky start with the church in Corinth—a badly-behaving bunch of believers that George G. Hunter III, in his book *Radical*

If we conclude that Jesus really is what he said, said what he meant, and meant what he said, then we'll have enough agenda to last us a lifetime.

> *God is not only saving the world. God is also saving the church.*

Outreach, classifies as "a dysfunctional church, with a mission." And sadly, things all too often in subsequent centuries only went further downhill from there.

The argument I frequently hear goes something like this: "The message of Jesus is probably a good one, but the church has done a ton of damage in trying to communicate it. If that's what mission is, then forget it. The church should just lay aside this mission thing for awhile, and concentrate on getting its own act together. Maybe someday it will have something worth sharing with the world."

The point is well taken. It has never been more important for the church to do some serious reflecting, repenting, and reordering of its life and practices to bring them more into line with God's will and ways. But if by "getting its act together" we have in mind seeing a brilliant butterfly Body of Christ emerging from its second-class caterpillar cocoon anytime soon, we might as well consider the church's participation in God's mission out of question for the near future and, in fact, on permanent hold.

The church has never ever in all its history been a perfect model and messenger of God's big plan to save the world. That's what makes it all the more incredible that God should have chosen it in the first place to head up The Cosmic Project's department of communications.

God is not only saving the world. God is also saving the church. And the church's job is nothing more or less than to serve as a witness to that salvation. Whenever the church has done that faithfully, people begin to see and hear the possibility of "good news" for their own tattered lives. They find themselves ineffably drawn to the sweet sound of God's amazing grace. This has happened in today's world for over two billion people—roughly one-third of the earth's total population.

6. Bible or newspaper. Speaking of cocoons, it is almost impossible for the church to live out its calling when it insists on staying tucked away in hibernation. Hibernation is, of course, a nice place to be. It feels fuzzy, fetal, far and free from life's harms and dangers. And it certainly is true that for a season—maybe even a fairly long one—hibernation can play an important life function.

But it is *not* life's ultimate goal. That is why whenever God's people throughout holy history have become too inwardly focused on their own internal agenda, God has sent prophets and preachers with wake-up words to help get The Cosmic Project back on track. Thus, not surprisingly, reports the Old Testament prophet Isaiah (49:6):

> The Lord said to me, "I have a greater task for you . . .
> Not only will you restore to greatness the people of Israel . . . but I will also make you a light to the nations—
> so that all the world may be saved."

It is my impression that most vibrant Christians are actually converted twice in their lifetimes, not just *once*. The first stage of transformation happens when they are converted "from the world to Christ," when they turn their backs on the past and their faces toward Jesus, choosing at that moment to organize their lives and futures around him.

For some, that's all that ever happens. And this is indeed a great beginning. But Christians who fully understand Christ's claims on their lives will find themselves converting yet again, this time "from Christ back to the world," accompanied as they go by the One who promises to "be there always," into those places where God's Peace-Making Project is still unknown or little understood.

7. Gospel meets culture. Followers of Jesus, like William Wade Harris and countless others who take this assignment seriously, often put life and limb at risk. Risk, and even possible death, in no way surprise them, however, because they are . . . following Jesus. And they know full well what happened to him. For many Christians in today's global South, "martyrdom is not merely a subject for historical research," notes Philip Jenkins in *The Next Christendom*, "it is a real prospect." And, "as we move into the new century," he adds, "the situation is likely to get worse rather than better."

Jenkins' projections are probably right because a number of things happen when God's gospel plan encounters the cultures of our world. There is on one hand the *affirmation* of culture. Much that makes up the social fabric of a people is "continued" or "completed" in some richer, deeper sense, or new initiatives build on older patterns within the culture to "create" exciting new expressions never before seen or heard.

But there is also the *threat factor* that occurs when the gospel begins to "correct" certain cultural patterns or understandings that simply no longer fit with God's *shalom*-making agenda. When this happens, local believers may find themselves in the unenviable position of needing to make some hard choices between what their culture is telling them and where God's Project is headed.

8. People encounters. It is one thing when the liberating good news of the gospel encounters people within a given culture and frees them to become everything God intended them to be. It is quite another thing when God's "messengers" come crashing into a culture—especially one other than their own—and, with little regard or respect for local ways, begin crushing and coercing people of the host environment, or cloning them into replicas of their own cultural likeness.

We as gospel communicators need to be reminded that God is, after all, the Creator and Sustainer of the entire universe. And this same God has been busy working to bring about *shalom*, even in the most remote, hidden corners of this universe, long before we ever arrived on the scene.

We don't bring God up to speed when our plane lands on the runway in any part of God's creation. God has, in fact, been waiting patiently for us at the arrival gate, wondering why our flight was so seriously delayed. Our greatest challenge as undeserving recipients of God's peacemaking initiatives is to get *ourselves* up to speed with what God has already been doing in the many millennia prior to our arrival. And then we must determine, through prayer and discernment, in what ways we might participate in God's local efforts, already well under way.

Gerald R. McDermott, in his book *Can Evangelicals Learn from World Religions?* (pages 218-219), puts it this way:

> Learning about [other] religions and seeing how God has revealed His truths to people of other faiths shows that God is at work in more ways and lands and people than many of us had imagined. The God of most evangelicals has been too small. We have conceived of His presence and Spirit as alive only among Christians, but learning from the religions will show us that God's Spirit is active far more expansively than we have ever imagined. As John said, "The true light, which enlightens *everyone*, was coming into the world" (John 1:9).

> *We don't bring God up to speed when our plane lands on the runway in any part of God's creation. God has, in fact, been waiting patiently for us at the arrival gate, wondering why our flight was so seriously delayed.*

9. Global faith family. When Christians fail to see and appreciate this bigger picture of what God is up to in the world, they begin to equate their own cultural patterns and understandings with The Cosmic Project itself. When this happens, cultural cloning—passed off as gospel communication—is almost certain to be lurking just around the corner.

We as Western messengers of the gospel have struggled with this issue for many years. There have been times when we succeeded in distinguishing between God's Grand Plan for all people and our own cultural version of it. And when we haven't, Professor B. Makhathini of the University of Swaziland reminds us what has been the unfortunate result:

> Before the bread of life (the Christian faith) came to our part of Africa, it stayed in Europe for over a thousand years. There the Europeans added a plastic bag (their own customs) to the bread. And when they came to Southern Africa, they fed us the bag along with the bread. Now, the plastic bag is making us sick! The plastic is theirs. We know that God planned for us to receive the bread just as he planned for them to receive it. We can remove the plastic, and enjoy the bread.

Enjoying the bread. Without the plastic. That is what increasing millions of people around the world are doing each day as the true light of Jesus shines into their lives and then out from there to their neighbors and friends around them.

Today, a large majority of the world Christian family lives in the global South, in Africa, Latin America, and Asia. The time has long since come for us Western Christians to wake up to this radically-changed reality and, in our relationships with these new members of our extended family, to begin moving with great dispatch:

- from parent to partner
- from lecturer to learner
- from resource to recipient
- from founder to friend.

There are recent reports of a vision among Chinese Christians to send 100,000 missionaries "back to Jerusalem" in the next 10 years. Just as the gospel originated in Jerusalem and spread from there in a variety of directions, these Christians believe that God is calling them today to complete the circle by taking the gospel from China in the East through Buddhist, Hindu, Muslim, and Jewish cultures, back to Jerusalem where the whole story began.

These believers anticipate resistance and possible imprisonment. Their preparation for the assignment includes training in things like "how to break free from hand-cuffs in thirty seconds" and "how to jump from second-story buildings without breaking a leg."

This kind of intensity with regards to God's mission comes across as almost bizarre to us Westerners. We have long since "cooled our heels" to any kind of religious activity requiring that much passion and commitment. Whether or not we agree with the vision and strategies of this par-

ticular initiative, there are clearly reasons why the church in the global South is growing at such a rapid pace. And why the church in the West is not.

A few words to close the book . . . and begin the journey

"It's a fairly embarrassing situation," writes Bruce H. Hargon, astrophysicist at the University of Washington, "to admit that we can't find 90 percent of the universe." That's the kind of humility it takes when you're writing a book about God's Cosmic Project to set things right with the world.

The fact is there are just lots of things about God's will and ways we don't fully comprehend. Even for those of us who believe, as I do, that Jesus Christ is both the greatest idea and the most decisive event in human history, that

> *There are clearly reasons why the church in the
> global South is growing at such a rapid pace.
> And why the church in the West is not.*

"simple" statement is already inexhaustible in meaning. As the apostle Paul tells us, Christ is "God's great mystery" through whom "all things hold together" and in whom "all the richest treasures of wisdom and knowledge are embedded" (Colossians 1:17; 2:2, 3, *The Message*).

If it is true that all reality is somehow comprehended in and by Christ, there is then, as George R. McDermott reminds us, "an infinite number of aspects or vantage points from which to see the idea of Christ, each of which will show something new and unique about what it means for God to be in Christ. This also means that as a church," McDermott adds, "we may have only begun the journey of understanding Christ, that there may be far more to Christ that the church will learn as it reflects on Scriptures and tradition—and perhaps other religions—with the help of the Holy Spirit" (page 16).

None of this alters in my mind, however, the central fact that God has done something in Jesus that the world deserves to know. Lesslie Newbigin, life-long missionary and former bishop in the Church of South India, takes it a step further when he writes:

> If, in fact, it is true that almighty God, creator and sustainer of all that exists in heaven or on earth, has—at a known time and place in human history—so humbled himself as to become part of our sinful humanity and to suffer and die a shameful death to take away our sin and to rise from the dead as the first-

> *Living with God's people for the past 30 years in seven ministry locations and on three continents has enriched my life and understandings beyond imagination.*

fruit of a new creation; if this is a fact, then to affirm it is not arrogance. To remain quiet about it is treason to our fellow human beings (1988: 328).

Living with God's people for the past 30 years in seven ministry locations and on three continents has enriched my life and understandings beyond imagination. Above all, it has provided a window for me to see God at work, gathering together a new family in Christ from around the world. Participating in the life of this family and encouraging others to consider joining it have become my principal passions in life. All other preoccupations appear insignificant to me, of little lasting value, and ultimately unworthy of the time and energies God has generously placed at my disposal.

It has taken me many years to arrive at such convictions. When I began my international experience in 1976 on the heels of Vietnam and in the heat of the U.S. Bicentennial hoopla, I was more than ready to leave behind the cultural arrogance and ethnocentrism my country had come to represent. I was ready to embrace what I hoped might be more laudable cultural patterns and values found elsewhere in God's world.

At one level, my expectations have been more than met. For in each place I have been privileged to live, my life has been richly blessed by aspects of local culture sadly missing in my own.

At another level, however, I have been witness in each of these same places to the backside of human existence, to mischief and greed, to abuse and injustice, to suffering brought on by individual and collective egotism of every insidious variety possible. With time, I have come to accept the rather pessimistic assessment of one observer who unmasks for us the true nature of our world and its cultural values. "The differences between Western culture and other cultures," he says, "is that in the West, human beings exploit other human beings, whereas elsewhere in the world, it is the other way around."

And yet . . . in the midst of what sometimes seems a helpless situation, I have found hope. This is the hope that comes from meeting men and women, brothers and sisters in Christ, inspired and driven by a larger vision for the world God has so loved. In this vision, lives are transformed, slaves to oppression and obsession find liberating release, and ancient walls of prejudice and hate are trampled under foot as people encounter the crucified-resurrected Lord.

I am sometimes asked by people my age and younger how in this world I can be committed to something as messy as mission. I believe it is time we ask how in a place as messy as this world we can legitimately be committed to anything *but* mission.

> *I am sometimes asked by people my age and younger how in this world I can be committed to something as messy as mission. I believe it is time we ask how in a place as messy as this world we can legitimately be committed to anything but mission.*

Not our own *personal* mission, you understand. Nor some kind of narrow *tribal* or *nationalistic* mission. (We all know well enough what distortions result from such initiatives.) But *God's* mission, God's Cosmic Project, veiled in mystery since the beginning of time, but now made clearer to us in the life and work of Jesus.

It is this mission alone, I believe, that is worthy of our time and energies. For it is this alone—in the words of a popular tune by a Nigerian Christian singer-composer—that can produce true "peace in our hearts, peace in our homes, peace in the nation and the world."

FOR FURTHER READING

AIKMAN, David, *Jesus in Beijing* (Washington, DC: Regnery Publishing, Inc., 2003).

BARRETT, Lois, ed., *Mission-Focused Congregations: A Bible Study* (Scottdale, Pa.: Faith and Life Resources, 2002).

BECKWITH, Francis J., and KOUKL, Gregory, *Relativism* (Grand Rapids, Mich.: Baker Books, 1998).

BERGER, Peter L., ed., *The Desecularization of the World* (Grand Rapids, Mich.: William B. Eerdmans, 1999).

BRADSHAW, Bruce, *Bridging the Gap: Evangelism, Development and* Shalom (Monrovia, Calif.: MARC, 1993).

CHANDLER, Paul-Gordon, *God's Global Mosaic: What We Can Learn from Christians around the World* (Downers Grove, Ill.: InterVarsity Press, 2000).

CLAPP, Rodney, *A Peculiar People: The Church as Culture in a Post-Christian Society* (Downers Grove, Ill.: InterVarsity Press, 1996).

CLENDENIN, Daniel B., *Many Gods, Many Lords* (Grand Rapids, Mich.: Baker Books, 1995).

HIEBERT, Paul G., *Anthropological Insights for Missionaries* (Grand Rapids, Mich.: Baker Book House, 1985).

HINES, Samuel George, and DeYOUNG, Curtiss Paul, *Beyond Rhetoric: Reconciliation as a Way of Life* (Valley Forge, Pa.: Judson Press, 2000).

HOLLINGER, Dennis P., *Head, Heart, and Hands* (Downers Grove, Ill.: InterVarsity Press, 2005).

HUNTER III, George G., *How to Reach Secular People* (Nashville, Tenn.: Abingdon Press, 1992).

_____, *Radical Outreach* (Nashville, Tenn.: Abingdon Press, 2003).

JENKINS, Philip, *The Next Christendom* (New York: Oxford University Press, 2002).

KRABILL, James R., *The Hymnody of the Harrist Church Among the Dida of South-Central Ivory Coast (1913-1949): A Historico-Religious Study* (Frankfurt/M.: Peter Lang GmbH, 1995).

MAUSER, Ulrich, *The Gospel of Peace* (Louisville, Ky.: Westminster/John Knox Press, 1992).

McDERMOTT, Gerald R., *Can Evangelicals Learn from World Religions?* (Downers Grove, Ill.: InterVarsity Press, 2000).

MUCK, Terry C., *Those Other Religions in Your Neighborhood* (Grand Rapids, Mich.: Zondervan Publishing House, 1992).

NEWBIGIN, Lesslie, "A Sermon Preached at the Thanksgiving Service for the Fiftieth Anniversary of the Tambaram Conference of the International Missionary Council," *International Review of Mission* 78 (1988), pp. 325-331.

_____, *The Gospel in a Pluralistic Society* (Grand Rapids, Mich.: Eerdmans, 1989).

NIDA, Eugene A., *Religion Across Cultures* (Pasadena, Calif.: William Carey Library, 1968).

OTT, Bernhard, *God's Shalom Project* (Intercourse, Pa: Good Books, 2004).

PELIKAN, Jaroslav, *Jesus through the Centuries* (New York: Harper & Row, 1985).

RAMACHANDRA, Vinoth, *Faiths in Conflict?* (Downers Grove, Ill.: InterVarsity Press, 1999).

RAMSEYER, Robert L., ed., *Mission and the Peace Witness* (Scottdale, Pa.: Herald Press, 1979).

SARDAR, Ziauddin, and DAVIES, Merryl Wyn, *Why Do People Hate America?* (Cambridge, England: Icon Books, 2003).

SHANK, David A., *Prophet Harris, the "Black Elijah" of West Africa* (Leiden, Netherlands: Brill, 1994).

_____, *What Western Christians Can Learn from African-Initiated Churches* (Elkhart, Ind.: Mennonite Board of Missions, 2001).

SIDER, Ronald J., *Cup of Water, Bread of Life* (Grand Rapids, Mich.: Zondervan Publishing House, 1994).

_____, *Genuine Christianity* (Grand Rapids, Mich.: Zondervan Publishing House, 1996).

_____, *One-Sided Christianity?* (Grand Rapids, Mich.: Zondervan Publishing House, 1993).

SNYDER, Howard A., *The Problem of Wine Skins* (Downers Grove, Ill.: InterVarsity Press, 1975).

STARK, Rodney, *The Rise of Christianity* (San Francisco: Harper, 1997).

STROHMER, Charles, *The Gospel and the New Spirituality* (Nashville: Thomas Nelson Publishers, 1996).

TIESSEN, Terrance L., *Who Can Be Saved? Reassessing Salvation in Christ and World Religions* (Downers Grove, Ill.: InterVarsity Press, 2004).

TWISS, Richard, *One Church, Many Tribes* (Ventura, Calif.: Regal Books, 2000).

WILKINS, Michael J., and MORELAND, J.P., eds., *Jesus under Fire* (Grand Rapids: Zondervan Publishing House, 1995).

YODER, Perry B., *Shalom: The Bible's Word for Salvation, Justice and Peace* (Nappanee, Ind.: Evangel Publishing House, 1987).

YOHANNAN, K. P., *Revolution in World Missions* (Carrollton, TX: GFA Books, 2000; first published by Creation House, 1986).

_____, *Why the World Waits: Exposing the Reality of Modern Missions* (Lake Mary, Fl.: Creation House, 1991).

ABOUT THE AUTHOR

James R. Krabill with his wife, Jeanette, served with Mennonite Board of Missions (MBM) over a period of 20 years (1976-1996). For much of this time, he was a Bible and church history teacher among African-initiated churches in West Africa. During the last four of those years, he was West Africa Director for MBM's program throughout a six-country region.

Krabill's doctoral dissertation in African hymnody from the University of Birmingham (U.K.) focused on the collection and analysis of several hundred Africa indigenous hymn texts. The study was published under the title: *The Hymnody of the Harrist Church Among the Dida of South-Central Ivory Coast, 1913-1949* (Peter Lang, 1995). More recent publications have included *The Short-Term Experience: Current Trends/ Future Challenges, Does Your Church "Smell" Like Mission?* and *Anabaptism and Mission,* a bibliography co-edited with Chad Mullet Bauman featuring 3,250 titles of Anabaptist/Mennonite writings on mission-related themes.

From 1995-2002, Krabill provided oversight to MBM's Mission Advocacy and Communication division, and, since then, has served as Senior Executive for Global Ministries at Mennonite Mission Network, the mission agency of Mennonite Church, USA. For his role in "churchwide ministry" he was ordained by his denomination in October 2003.

Krabill and his wife have three adult children, Matthew, Elisabeth, and Mary Laura, all born in Abidjan, Ivory Coast, and all currently living in Philadelphia, Pennsylvania.